U0772618

晚清美国驻华公使柔克义
涉藏档案选编

Selected Documents Relating to Tibet
from William W. Rockhill Papers

程 龙

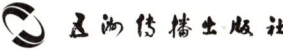
五洲传播出版社

图书在版编目（CIP）数据

晚清美国驻华公使柔克义涉藏档案选编 / 程龙编著 .

—— 北京：五洲传播出版社，2016.8

ISBN 978-7-5085-3510-4

Ⅰ . ①晚… Ⅱ . ①程… Ⅲ . ①中美关系－西藏问题－

国际关系史－史料－清后期 Ⅳ . ① D829.712

中国版本图书馆 CIP 数据核字 (2016) 第 196365 号

晚清美国驻华公使柔克义涉藏档案选编

编　　著：程　龙

设计制作：北京正视文化艺术有限责任公司

责任编辑：宋博雅　姜　超

出版发行：五洲传播出版社

社　　址：北京市北三环中路 31 号生产力大楼 B 座 6 层

邮　　编：100088

网　　址：http://www.cicc.org.cn

电　　话：0086-10-82007837（发行部）

印　　刷：北京久佳印刷有限责任公司

开　　本：787 毫米 ×1092 毫米　1/16

印　　张：12

印　　数：1—3000

字　　数：186 千字

版　　次：2016 年 8 月第 1 版第 1 次印刷

定　　价：42.00 元

Contents
目录

Preface
前言

柔克义（William W. Rockhill，1853—1913）是 19 世纪末到 20 世纪初美国的著名外交官，他曾在 1884 到 1888 年间担任美国驻华使馆秘书，1900 到 1901 年曾以美国总统特使身份来华签订《辛丑条约》；1905 到 1909 年间，他担任美国驻大清帝国的最高外交代表——美国驻华公使。柔克义也是著名的探险家、汉学家和藏学家，在不算长的 60 年生命历程中，有 10 年多是在中国度过的，并完成了大量汉学和藏学研究著述，获得了很高的学术声誉。

作为第一个进入西藏的美国人和当时为数不多的藏学家，他既是晚清时期美国对华（涉藏）政策的重要制定者，也是对华关系（涉藏事务）的积极参与者和实践者。

20 世纪初，美国的对华外交政策是著名的"门户开放"原则（Open Door Policy），这一政策为美国在西藏主权归属问题上的态度奠定了基础，而柔克义恰好是"门户开放"政策的主要倡导者和积极推动者之一。1899 年，美国取得美西战争的胜利后夺取了西班牙在菲律宾的殖民地，由此将扩张的触角伸到亚洲。此时的中国正经历着甲午战败后的各种危机，面临被西方列强瓜分的威胁。当时担任助理国务卿的柔克义在与英国汉学家贺璧理通信的过程中首先提出了"门户开放"政策，并将其作为美国亚洲外交政策的建议提供给国务卿海约翰（John Hay）。1899 年 12 月，海约翰向西方列强发出照会，正式提出了"门户开放"政策。这项政策得到了英、法、德、俄、日等西方列强的接受和认可。这项政策从根本上说是为了维护美国在中国的利益，它要求西方各国在中国"机会均等、利益均沾"，从而使姗姗来迟的美国可以在欧洲列强的势力范围中分一杯羹。但另一方面，这项政策也为欧美列强设定了一个前提，那就是中国的领土和行政完整必须得到有效的保证，任何西方列强不得向中国提出领土要求，中国不能被分割和肢解。"门户开放"政策的完整表述是：

美国政府的政策是谋求一解决办法，以便达到：给中国带来永久的安全与和平；保证中国领土和行政完整；保护友邦经条约和国际法所承认的所有权利；保证世界与中国各地平等公正贸易的原则。

The policy of the Government of the United States is to seek a solution which may bring about permanent safety and peace for China, preserve Chinese territorial and administrative entity, protect all rights guaranteed to friendly powers by treaty and international law, and safeguard for the world the principle of equal and impartial trade with all parts of Chinese empire. *(Foreign Relations of the United States,* 1900, p.299*)*

正是在"门户开放"政策的背景下，美国政府强调中国在开放门户的同时，西方各国不应破坏中国的领土完整。秉承"门户开放"政策，在对待列强争夺西藏态度上，美国的立场是反对英国、俄国独占西藏或把西藏分裂出去的企图，承认中国中央政府对西藏的管辖。柔克义更是这一立场的坚定执行者。他始终坚持认为"西藏是中国不可分割的一部分"，"西藏应服从中央政府"，并在与十三世达赖喇嘛会面以及与美国总统西奥多·罗斯福的通信中清晰完整地表达了这一观点。虽然从本质上说，柔克义是为了维护美国在华利益而提出上述观点的，但这一结论也符合历史事实。

柔克义的一生紧密地和中国联系在一起。从青少年时代自学藏语和汉语开始，到 1884 年首度作为美国驻华公使馆秘书到北京工作；从 19 世纪 80 年代末考察西藏，到 1900 年作为美国总统特使参与义和团之后与清政府的谈判；从 1905 年担任美国驻大清帝国的最高外交代表——驻华公使，到与十三世达赖喇嘛数度会面斡旋西藏危机；等等。他亲历了中国近代史上的很多重大事件，更在其中发挥了重要作用。他跟美国政坛上的风云人物西奥多·罗斯福总统、国务卿海约翰以及美国第二任总统约翰·亚当斯的曾孙亨利·亚当斯（Henry Adams）都是极为要好的朋友；

他跟慈禧太后、光绪皇帝、十三世达赖喇嘛、李鸿章、庆亲王奕劻、张之洞、袁世凯、刘坤一、伍廷芳、唐绍仪等清末民初中国权力的持有者们都有过面对面的直接接触。1914 年，60 岁的柔克义接受北洋政府的邀请担任外交顾问一职，再度启程前往中国。行至檀香山，柔克义突发心脏病去世。

鉴于柔克义在美国外交史以及中美关系上的重要地位以及他在汉学和藏学领域较高的学术声誉，柔克义涉藏档案值得深入研究，其历史价值也值得深入挖掘。

2013 到 2014 年，我先后三次赴美国哈佛大学、耶鲁大学、美国国会图书馆、美国国家档案馆、史密森学会博物馆等地，对保存在各地的柔克义涉藏档案进行了整理研究。研究完成后，中国藏学研究中心张云研究员、梁俊艳副研究员，中央党校胡岩教授等对报告提出了宝贵的修改意见。

本书分三个部分介绍"柔克义档案整理与研究"的情况：一、柔克义对西藏的研究与游历；二、"柔克义涉藏档案"的基本情况、历史价值和现实意义；三、"柔克义涉藏档案"选编。

程龙

2016 年 5 月

William W. Rockhill

① 柔克义对西藏的研究与游历

Rockhill's Travels in Tibet and His Tibetan Studies

柔克义之所以积极关注并参与晚清西藏事务，是由于他青少年时代对西藏产生了很大兴趣，一直从事藏学研究并亲自到西藏游历考察；他有关西藏的政治及学术观点之所以产生巨大的影响力，是由于他在学术研究和地理考察方面作出了重要贡献。因此，了解柔克义对西藏的研究和游历，对于正确把握其"涉藏文献"的历史价值和现实意义是十分必要的。

一、柔克义青年时代的藏学研究

柔克义 1853 年 4 月 1 日出生在美国宾夕法尼亚州的一个律师家庭，幼年时因美国爆发南北战争，举家迁往法国巴黎。1872 年，柔克义进入法国圣居尔军事学院学习。正是在法国侨居求学期间，他读到了法国传教士古伯察（Régis-Évariste Huc，1813—1860）于 1850 年出版的《鞑靼西藏旅行记》[1]。这本书开启了柔克义对雪域高原的美好憧憬和向往，西藏也从此成为他一生不懈去探索追求的目标。从此，柔克义开始自学藏语。巴黎的"法兰西学院"作为当时西方亚洲研究的中心为柔克义提供了良好的学习环境，他得以接触到大量有关中国语言文化的书籍。很快，柔克义发现，要想真正学好藏语和藏学，还要学会汉语，他又开始了自学汉语的历程。在 20 多岁的青年时代，柔克义便掌握了英、法、汉、藏四门语言，这为他后来的外交生涯和学术研究都奠定了坚实的基础。

从军校毕业后，柔克义以外国雇佣兵的身份被分配到法国在北非的殖民地阿尔及利亚服役。军校和军队生涯锻炼了他的体魄和胆识，也教会了他如何使用武器、指南针和各种测量仪器并提高了他在野外生存的技能，这些知识和经验对于他后来的两次西藏探险都具有重大意义。

1876 年，柔克义返回美国成婚。由于没有固定工作，为生活

---

[1]　古伯察 1839 年来到中国传教，1841 年抵达北京。1844 年 8 月，古伯察和他的上司秦噶呲（Joseph Gabet，1808—1853）神甫从河北出发，途经热河、蒙古诸旗、鄂尔多斯、宁夏、甘肃、青海、西康地区，历经 18 个月的艰苦旅行，最终于 1846 年 1 月 29 日到达西藏首府拉萨。在拉萨停留两个月后，他们被清政府驱逐出藏，经四川、湖北、江西等地抵达澳门。古伯察将他在旅行中的所见所闻写成了《鞑靼西藏旅行记》（*Souvenirs d'un Voyage Dans La Tartarie*），记述了他从内蒙古黑水川出发进入西藏到被清政府驱逐至康定的全过程。这本书于 1850 年首次在巴黎面世。1854 年，古伯察将从康定到澳门的经历写成《中华帝国——鞑靼西藏旅行记续》（*L'Empire Chinois：Faisant Suite A L'Ouvrage Intitulé Souvenirs d'un Voyage Dans La Tartarie*）在法国出版。

所迫，他带着新婚妻子举家到美国西南的德克萨斯州去开办农场，加入了西部开发的洪流。在养牛之余，柔克义仍然没有放弃学习藏语和汉语，并开始了他的学术研究工作。巴黎法兰西学院的朋友们仍不间断地将各种中文和藏文书籍资料邮寄给他，繁重的农场工作并没有影响到他对亚洲语言和宗教的兴趣。

1880 年，美国东方学会（American Oriental Society）破天荒地接受了柔克义这位牛仔成为会员，并在当年于纽约召开的会员大会上宣读了他的论文《佛说四十二章经（译自藏文）》（The Sûtra in Forty-two Chapters, translated from Tibetan），《美国东方学会会报》（Journal of American Oriental Society）刊登了论文的提要介绍 [1]。这是柔克义第一次公开发表藏学研究论文，虽然以翻译为主，但至少说明他的研究已经达到了一定水平，引起了美国学术界的注意。

1881 年，柔克义对大乘佛教典籍《金刚经》的藏文版进行了研究，发现早期佛教经典语言质朴简略，并没有后来不断增加的各种华丽修饰。藏文版《金刚经》更接近梵文原本，比其中文译本简要得多。1881 年 5 月，美国东方学会在波士顿召开大会，柔克义关于大乘佛教典籍的研究论文又一次在大会上被宣读。柔克义在文中指出：《金刚经》自传入中国后便有两个较为流行的译本，一为鸠摩罗什译本，一为玄奘译本，英国佛教专家毕尔在 1864 年曾将玄奘本《金刚经》翻译成英文 [2]，随后他将鸠摩罗什的译本也译成英文，二者在字数和内容上都有不小的区别。柔克义在法国巴黎国家图书馆找到了一份梵文《金刚经》的原本，经

---

[1] Proceedings at New York, Oct. 28th, 1880, *Journal of American Oriental Society*, Vol.11, 1885, p. l.

[2] Samuel Beal, *Histoire de la Vie et des Voyages de Hiouen Thsang*, J. R. A. S, New Series, Vol. i., p. 30.

过和藏文版比对，他发现仅有 18 页的藏文版《金刚经》比起鸠摩罗什或者玄奘的中译本更加接近梵文原文 [1]。

由于柔克义把主要精力都用于藏学研究，他经营的农场日益惨淡，最终不得不放弃。柔克义带着妻子和女儿移居到瑞士投靠他的母亲。在瑞士寓居期间，柔克义的藏学研究不但没有中断，反而取得了接二连三的成果。

1883 年，柔克义在伦敦出版了一部藏文佛经的译文，这是他的第一部专著，题目是《〈法句经〉——佛经偈颂选集》（*Udanavarga: A Collection of Verses from the Buddhist Canon*）[2]。柔克义在对《四十二章经》进行研究后，立刻对《法句经》产生了兴趣。因为《四十二章经》跟《法句经》有密切的渊源关系。不过，他的视角从汉文、藏文《法句经》的对勘扩展为巴利文、藏文《法句经》的对比校勘。这种变化不仅仅是文本的转换，柔克义敏锐意识到了其中更深层次的内涵，将《法句经》巴利文本与藏文本进行比较，并辅以中文本，无形中是在比较南传佛教与北传佛教典籍之间的异同，从而比较南北佛教传播的差异。柔克义在对比研究中所采用的正是吴本《法句经》的巴利文母本，他在这本书的封面上实际已经表明了写作目的，该书的副标题是"佛经选集，法救（Dharmastrata）编，即南传《法句经》（*Dhammapada*）的北传佛教版本，译自甘珠尔（Bkah-hgyur）的藏文"[3]。

1884 年 6 月，他在瑞士洛桑完成了一部新书的手稿，名字叫《佛

---

[1]　Proceedings at Boston, May 18th, 1881, *Journal of American Oriental Society,* Vol.11, 1885, p. lxvi.

[2]　William W. Rockhill, *Udanavarga: A Collection of Verses from the Buddhist Canon*, London: Trubner & Co, 1883.

[3]　William W. Rockhill, *Udanavarga: A Collection of Verses from the Buddhist Canon*, London: Trubner & Co, 1883. Front Cover.

陀传——源自藏文文献甘珠尔（Bkah-hgyur）和丹珠尔（Bstan-hgyur）的关于佛陀的早期历史》（*The Life of the Buddha*）。西方学者对大藏经的介绍和研究始于匈牙利著名藏学专家乔玛（Alexander Csoma de Koros，1784—1842）。柔克义受其启发开始关注大藏经研究，但柔克义认为乔玛的时代"还处于藏学研究的初始阶段，《甘珠尔》对藏学很多重要问题的解答还没有被学者们发现，而它的重要意义也被忽略"[1]。

同一年，柔克义还在《美国东方学会会报》上发表了《米拉日巴十万歌集》（*The Tibetan Hundred Thousand Songs of Milaraspa, A Buddhist Missionary of Eleventh Century*）一文[2]。米拉日巴，出生于公元1040年，曾拜西藏四大教派之一的噶举派始祖玛尔巴为师，1123年去世。"他在宗教方面，是一个道德高尚、性行纯洁的高僧，反对喇嘛僧众贪取金钱财物，自害害人。在西藏佛教中受到普遍的尊重，称之为至尊"[3]。米拉日巴自幼喜欢唱歌，是一位著名的宗教诗人。他的诗歌集叫作《十万歌集》，是最先拥有专集的藏族诗人。这部诗集是米拉日巴的弟子为他编撰的，其中某些章节后有"弟子某某记录"的字样。柔克义首先回顾了米拉日巴生活时代的历史背景以及他和噶举派始祖玛尔巴的关系，然后指出"与米拉日巴相关的文献有两部，一是《十万歌集》，一是《米拉日巴传》"[4]。中国学者分析过《十万歌集》的内容[5]，但从未介绍过该书的版本。柔克义将他用来研究的《十万

---

[1] William W. Rochill, *The Life of the Buddha,* London: Trubner & Co, 1884, Introduction, p. v.

[2] Proceedings at Baltimore, Oct. 29th, 1884, *Journal of American Oriental Society*, Vol.11, 1885, p. ccvii.

[3] 王沂暖、唐景福：《藏族文学史略（三）》，《西北民族学院学报》1983年第1期。

[4] Proceedings at Baltimore, Oct. 29th, 1884, *Journal of American Oriental Society*, Vol.11, 1885, p. ccvii.

[5] 王沂暖、唐景福：《藏族文学史略（三）》，《西北民族学院学报》1983年第1期。

歌集》寄给美国东方学会，据他描述，这本《十万歌集》"共有
60 章 245 页，其中一部分为刊本，一部分为稿本。……其语言与
我们在经典佛经中看到的完全不同，值得深入研究"[1]。柔克义
在文章中从音节的角度举例分析了《十万歌集》的语言学特点。
这是迄今为止中外学者对《十万歌集》最为深入的研究之一。对
《十万歌集》的研究反映出柔克义的研究范围已经从藏文佛教经
典扩展到藏文文学领域，当然，他关注的焦点仍然是语言学分析
以及多语种之间的对比校勘。这种研究兴趣的扩展在欧洲藏学家
中是很普遍的，柔克义似乎也秉承了这一倾向，逐渐开始关注藏
文文学。

柔克义的藏学研究引起了美国学界和政界的注意，很多人在
拜读了他的著述后主动和他建立联系，请教问题并成为朋友。
柔克义把他"想去中国看看"的想法告诉了这些学术界和政界
的朋友，他在一封信中写道：

多年以来，我一直觉得只有生活在亚洲才能充分进行我的东方
研究。在那里我可以和说这种语言、信仰这种宗教的人一起交流，
我对这种语言和宗教十分感兴趣。我想到美国驻北京公使馆去工作，
而不是更多地呆在美国，我不知道有什么办法能实现这个想法，如
您能提些建议，我将感激不尽[2]。

在很多热情友人的帮助下，年届 30 岁的柔克义在 1884 年接
到了被任命为美国驻北京公使馆二等秘书的通知。他于当年 9 月

---

[1]　Proceedings at Baltimore, Oct. 29th, 1884, *Journal of American Oriental Society*, Vol.11, 1885, p. ccvii.

[2]　WWR to Whitney, Aug. 17th, 1883. Whitney Papers.

抵达北京，开始了他的外交生涯。

在北京担任外交官期间，柔克义也没有间断他对藏学的研究和关注。他经常请在北京的藏传佛教喇嘛去公使馆教他藏文、讨论藏学。他也和到访北京的其他藏学家建立广泛的联系和交流，例如 1885 年他和印度藏学家达斯相见后便成了学术上的重要知己。

1885 年春天，英印政府派出了一个以马科蕾（Colman Macaulay）为首的使团到北京访问，目的是说服清政府同意英国在西藏设立领事馆，这一目标最终未能实现。因为交涉的议题涉及西藏事务，使团中特意安排了一位藏学专家担任顾问，这是一个名叫萨拉特·钱德拉·达斯（Sarat Chandra Das）的孟加拉人。达斯是西方颇负盛名的藏学家，不但精通藏语，还有着丰富的西藏考察经验。1878 年，他在一位锡金喇嘛的陪同下首次进入西藏探险。在西藏滞留的 6 个月时间里，他虽然未能到达拉萨，却在日喀则见到了班禅喇嘛。

达斯在西藏之行中不但偷偷绘制了西藏沿路的地形图，记录了道路状况，获取了西藏的一些社会人文情报，还盗走了许多价值连城的藏文、梵文典籍。这些文献成为他学术成就的重要基础，他后来发表的许多关于藏族语言文字、历史、文化、宗教等方面的论著都以引用当时外间罕见的藏文资料而受到国外学者的重视[1]。

1881 年，达斯再次入藏，这次他在西藏滞留的时间长达 14 个月，还成功到达拉萨并会见了年仅 8 岁的十三世达赖喇嘛。返回印度后，达斯撰写了第二次西藏考察的旅行报告《拉萨及西藏

---

[1] 冯蒸：《国外西藏研究概况：1949—1978》，中国社会科学出版社，1986 年，第 3 页。

中部旅行记》（*Journey to Lhasa and Central Tibet*）[1]，这部书的内容在很长时间内被英印政府当作绝密资料保存，直到 1902 年才正式出版发行。除此以外，达斯还编撰了享誉国际藏学界的《藏英词典》（*Tibetan-English Dictionary*），有些中国学者评价，"这是继匈牙利人乔玛和德国人耶司克各自编撰的藏英词典之后在该领域最大规模的辞书，直到 1985 年张怡孙主编的《藏汉大辞典》出版以后，该辞典在藏文辞书领域的领先地位才结束"[2]。实际上，《藏汉大辞典》毕竟是藏语和汉语之间相互转换的工具书，仍然无法取代达斯《藏英词典》的地位。

1885 年达斯访问北京时，《拉萨及西藏中部旅行记》以及《藏英词典》都尚未出版，他还不是 20 年之后那个藏学界家喻户晓的人物。但此时他已经成功完成了两次西藏考察，其丰富的西藏旅行经验正是柔克义所看重的。柔克义很快通过英国驻华公使馆跟这位志同道合的朋友建立了联系。达斯在北京期间跟柔克义的交往频繁而密切。1885 年 10 月，柔克义应邀到英国公使馆做关于西藏问题的讲座，达斯也作为嘉宾出席。柔克义甚至考虑和达斯一起去西藏考察，达斯也非常高兴地接受了柔克义的邀请。返回印度后，他给柔克义写信说，"关于我们旅行的伟大计划，我不改初衷。我要完成这个伟大而又危险的任务的希望丝毫不减"[3]。尽管柔克义和达斯一起考察西藏的愿望后来未能实现，但很显然，柔克义从达斯那里得到了不少关于西藏的信息，这对他后来的西藏之行大有裨益。

---

[1]　该书中译本由陈观胜、李培茱译，中国藏学出版社 2005 年出版。

[2]　肖杰：《印度主要涉藏研究机构及人员概况》，《中国藏学》2011 年第 2 期。

[3]　Das to WWR, Feb.6, 1886. Rockhill Papers.

在达斯离开北京后，柔克义和他保持了长久的通信，他们不但时常在学术上交流，也成为要好的朋友。1902 年，达斯出版《拉萨及西藏中部旅行记》时，柔克义为其撰写了序言并对全书进行了注释。1915 年，达斯出版《藏语语法》（*An Introduction to the Grammar of Tibetan Langue*）一书时特意把柔克义对达赖喇嘛的描述放在扉页之后，还摘抄了几段柔克义给自己的信件加以说明。可见，柔克义与达斯之间的友谊保持了 30 多年。对于达斯给自己的帮助，柔克义在《拉萨及西藏中部旅行记》序言中表达了感谢：

1885 年，印度政府考虑派一个使团到西藏去，于是派已故的可尊敬的科尔曼·麦考利到北京去，想取得中国政府对印度的这个计划中的使团的认可。萨拉特·钱德拉陪同科尔曼到中国首都去，在那里住了几个月。正是在他访问北京期间，我认识了这位印度绅士，他使我对藏学产生了终身的浓厚兴趣。在北京期间，萨拉特住在安定门外一个叫作西黄寺的喇嘛庙内。当时所有来北京的西藏商人都住在那里。……可是这个计划没有实现。从那以后，这位印度绅士在大吉岭期间以全部精力从事藏文书籍的出版工作和编撰有关佛教的著作 [1]。

我个人永远感谢他在北京期间为我提供的宝贵信息，这对我后来在西藏的探险有很大帮助。我认为自己特别幸运，被皇家地理学会选中来编辑他的西藏旅行报告，因为我可以借此来公开我对他的感激之情，并且我相信，我可以借此来帮助他作为与乔玛（Csoma

---

[1] [印]萨拉特·钱德拉·达斯著, [美]柔克义编：《拉萨及西藏中部旅行记》，柔克义导论, 中国藏学出版社 2005 年版，第 10 页。

de Koro）并驾齐驱的最伟大的赴西藏探险的先驱者，取得应当得到的地位[1]。

除了与藏学家接触外，柔克义还在北京担任外交官期间购买大量汉文和藏文书籍，为他的学术研究奠定了文献基础。

1888年，柔克义辞去了公使馆的职务，在美国史密森学会的支持下开始了他考察西藏的旅程。

二、柔克义对西藏的游历

在1888到1892的四年时间里，柔克义两度进入西藏考察，他终于实现了多年的夙愿。虽然两次旅行都没能抵达拉萨，但雪域高原上的亲身感受和多年积累的各种语言及文化知识呼应起来，感性认识让柔克义对西藏历史、地理和民族有了更深刻的理解。

1888年，柔克义开始了他的第一次西藏之旅。对于进藏的路线，柔克义有着自己的考虑：

欧洲旅行者通常从印度或者中国西部进入西藏，沿着这两个区域的边界人口稠密，或者说唯一穿过边界地区可通行的道路经过很多大的城镇和乡村，因此那些旅行者都发现他们在快要进入西藏的门槛时遇到很多障碍。那里生性多疑的居民把每一个想要访问该地区的陌生人都看作是危险的闯入者，其目的是盗窃这块土地所蕴含的丰富矿产或者是为侵略军前来探路。

---

[1] ［印］萨拉特·钱德拉·达斯著，［美］柔克义编：《拉萨及西藏中部旅行记》，柔克义导论，中国藏学出版社2005年版，第11页。

西藏北部是由许多条东西走向的山脉所分隔的高原。这里荒凉干旱，要么是沙漠，要么零星居住着一些游牧部落。在这些部落的南边而且只有在较大的山谷里才居住着耕种土地的居民。因此，看起来从北边来的旅行者就不会像从其他方向进入那样遇到当地居民强烈的反对，从而能在西藏走得更远。

　　这些考虑以及1845年古伯察和秦噶呲神甫从北部进入西藏的成功尝试，让我选择了这条道路作为我的考察之路。

　　1888年冬，在辞去了公使馆秘书一职后，我开始准备旅行。我所选择的是一条大路，经过西安府、兰州府到青海湖旁的西宁府，从那里开始才是通往西藏北部的道路[1]。

　　1888年12月17日，他和几个随从带着两辆骡车离开了北京，踏上了梦想多年的西藏之行。柔克义出发后，用了5个星期的时间通过中国北方抵达西宁。严格意义上说，这里已经是青藏高原了，西宁周边的藏族居民渐渐多起来。柔克义非常高兴，他第一次置身于藏民中间，感受他们的文化，了解他们的宗教，学习并使用他们的语言。柔克义对西宁以及柴达木盆地关注已久，他早就决定要从这里进入西藏，因此平日十分留心这里的情况。久负盛名的塔尔寺是柔克义早就听说过的，他抵达这里时正赶上展佛节。柔克义在这里逗留了6个星期，详细地考察寺庙的建筑、宗教节日活动及其周围居民的各种风土人情。

　　柴达木地区的藏民告诉柔克义，去拉萨的旅途困难重重，不但路途遥远，气候恶劣，沿途还有土匪活动。各种困难因素

---

[1]　William W. Rockhill, *The Land of the Lamas: Notes of a Journey through China, Mongolia and Tibet,* The Century Company, New York, 1891, pp.1-2.

大大减弱了柔克义的积极性，使他决定改变路线。柔克义放弃了拉萨，转而向藏东地区前进，希望经过昌都去印度的阿萨姆邦，或者从那里到四川打箭炉。1889 年 4 月，柔克义带着两个蒙古人、4 个汉人、17 匹马和两头藏獒经过青海湖北侧刚察的道路进入柴达木盆地，再转而向南途经都兰、巴隆，进入鄂陵湖地区并翻越巴颜喀拉山口。5 月 25 日，柔克义抵达今玉树藏族自治州首府结古，并从这里向东南方向经德格、甘孜到达四川打箭炉。

其实，真正让柔克义放弃目的地拉萨的，是他在柴达木盆地时听说有一个 75 人组成的俄国探险队去年冬天已经抵达了拉萨。这个消息后来被证明是错误的，但当时的柔克义深信不疑，因为就在几个月前的 1888 年 10 月，俄国地理学家、探险家普尔热瓦尔斯基开始了他的第 5 次中亚探险。虽然他在 10 月 20 日因感染伤寒而病逝，但柔克义相信，队伍中的其他人继续前进并抵达了拉萨。这样一来，柔克义觉得自己这次考察活动的意义大大打了折扣，即便他成功抵达拉萨，他也不是自古伯察和秦噶吡之后第一个到拉萨的西方人了，顶多算是第一个美国人罢了。

柔克义在打箭炉呆了两个星期，享受着法国传教士的热情招待，并搜集有关中国西南的信息。7 月 10 日他离开打箭炉，通过四川地区向东部沿海前进。他以英国领事馆客人的身份在重庆停留了 10 天，然后沿长江顺流而下，8 月 8 日，抵达宜昌，8 月 20 日，到达上海。在整整 8 个月中，柔克义走行 7500 公里，所经过的多为西方人不了解的区域。几年后，柔克义总结他的旅行时说道：

我在中国内地、蒙古和西藏旅行。我打扮成一个汉族边民，吃所有汉人、蒙古人和藏人吃的脏东西。我用手指而不是刀叉或者筷子。我把盘子舔干净而不是洗干净。我遵从所经过地区的社会习俗，我差一点饿死。有时候，我患上雪盲。我还要从藏东敌对喇嘛那里逃命[1]。

他在旅行当中除了细心观察之外，还带着各种仪器随时进行测量。柔克义还专门绘制了考察的线路图，附在他发表的有关这次旅行的文章和专著中。

所附的路线图是从我利用梭镜罗盘、沸点测高计和气压计所测量的1/4英寸比例尺地图上简化而来的。我不能说它是完全精确的，我在画图的时候十分认真，我相信它对于了解我所穿过这个区域的地形是有帮助的[2]。

自1890年11月起，柔克义开始在美国著名的《世纪》杂志上连载他有关西藏考察的文章：《一个美国人在西藏——穿越未知地域从华北到青海湖》[3]、《中国的边疆——一次穿越未知地域的旅行》[4]、《在蔚蓝色湖的蒙古人中间》[5]、《藏北与黄河》[6]、《穿

[1]   William W. Rockhill, Driven out of Tibet, *The Century,* April, 1894, p. 877.

[2]   William W. Rockhill, *The Land of the Lamas: Notes of a Journey through China, Mongolia and Tibet,* The Century Company, New York, 1891, Preface.

[3]   William W. Rockhill, An American in Tibet: An Account of a Journey through an Unknown Land, through Northern China to Koko-nor, The Century, Nov.1890-Mar. 1891.

[4]   William W. Rockhill, The Borderland of China: A Journey through an Unknown Land, *The Century,* Dec. 1890, pp.250-263.

[5]   William W. Rockhill, Among the Mongols of the Azure Lakes, *The Century,* Jan.1891, pp. 250-361.

[6]   William W. Rockhill, Northern Tibet and the Yellow River, *The Century,* Feb.1891, pp. 599-606.

越藏东与华中》[1] 等。这些文章为美国人打开了一个神秘的世界，那不为人知的雪域高原开始显露出她的面容。

从西藏回来以后，柔克义一直准备撰写一部游记以全面总结这次西藏之行，为《世纪》杂志所写的系列文章都可以看作是对这部书的前期准备。

我们现在可以通过 1891 年柔克义出版的《喇嘛之地》（*The Land of the Lamas: Notes of a Journey through China, Mongolia and Tibet*）一书来了解柔克义第一次西藏之行的全过程。柔克义在书的序言中写道："这本书的目的是提供关于这个地区的事实，历史的、地理的和民族的，而不是要写一部完美的文学作品。"[2] 因此，他在旅行中尽可能地观察，在书中尽可能地记述观察的记录，而不是个人感受。他还把多年研究西藏的知识运用起来，这使这部考察记的信息量十分巨大：

> 除了我在旅行中所搜集的记录之外，我在北京居住四年期间的工作以及我在西藏各地和甘肃边界跟当地人亲切的日常交谈都在很多方面使这部书得以完善。地理和考古方面的大量中文文献也对我有极大帮助，提供了大量信息，让我能够解释那些风俗习惯和专有名词。虽然这些信息并不都是正确的，但是总有参考价值[3]。

这本关于西藏的游记取名《喇嘛之地》，由美国世纪公司和

---

[1] William W. Rockhill, Through Eastern Tibet and Central China, *The Century,* Mar.1891, pp. 720-730.

[2] William W. Rockhill, *The Land of the Lamas: Notes of a Journey through China, Mongolia and Tibet,* The Century Company, New York, 1891, Preface.

[3] William W. Rockhill, *The Land of the Lamas: Notes of a Journey through China, Mongolia and Tibet,* The Century Company, New York, 1891, Preface.

英国朗曼格林公司联合出版。本书在前面介绍柔克义西藏之行时所引用的很多段落都来自这本游记。这本书共分 7 个部分，详细叙述了柔克义从北京出发，途经晋、陕、甘、青抵达西藏并经打箭炉到宜昌、上海的全过程，对西藏的社会、文化、宗教、语言和地理进行了全面介绍。

书的风格跟《世纪》杂志上发表的文章很相似，更关注于学术而不是个人经历。书中包含了将近 60 页的大量附录表格，不厌其烦地标注各个藏族部落的发音，这让很多读者感到头痛，但关心西藏语言、宗教、历史和地理的学者却十分高兴，把这本书当作是难得的珍贵资料。柔克义显然也在文风和内容上作了一些调整，以满足读者的好奇心。他在枯燥而严肃的学术研究中也插入了一些非同寻常和激动人心的经历，有些还不乏黑色幽默。为了吸引读者，书中还插入了大量反映西藏风土人情的铜版画，这些直观的视觉影像对于美国读者理解雪域高原至关重要。

这本书出版后立即产生了不小的影响，如代表了多数读者和学者观点的《大西洋月刊》（*Atlantic Monthly*）这样评价：

我们相信，他是第一个访问西藏的美国人，他的勇气值得我们尊敬，他的书对于地理学和人种学来说，价值非凡 [1]。

《喇嘛之地》不仅在美国产生了很大的反响，全世界的地理学家和探险家都注意到了这本关于西藏的游记。20 世纪最著名的中亚探险家、瑞典地理学家斯文·赫定很快就成了《喇嘛之地》

---

[1] *Atlantic Monthly*, May 1892, p. 691.

的读者，他在两年之后的 1893 年开始了自己的首次中亚和西藏探险。在前期准备当中，《喇嘛之地》是必读书，他必须了解前人已经做了哪些工作，还有什么未能解决的问题。而柔克义是最近一位到过西藏的西方人，斯文·赫定无疑要参考他的成果。后来，斯文·赫定在讲述自己多年的亚洲探险经历时指出，他对柔克义西藏旅行的情况非常了解。就像古伯察《鞑靼西藏旅行记》点燃了柔克义的东方梦想一样，《喇嘛之地》也引领着斯文·赫定走向中亚和神秘的雪域高原。斯文·赫定是一位非常挑剔、要求极为严格的探险家和地理学家，他很少赞扬同时代的其他同行，不过，他还是在 1898 年出版的《穿越亚洲》一书中高度评价了柔克义在西藏探险和研究方面的贡献：

> 1888 到 1889 年，美国人柔克义在藏东地区进行了一次旅行。从北京出发的时候，他只带了一个随从和几匹马，他行进至青海湖，穿越扬子江最终回到上海。他能够说汉语和藏语，并在旅行中进行了伪装。他完成了一流的地图测绘工作，测量了海拔高度，做了记录，还指出了以往欧洲地图在地形和水文方面的错误和不可信[1]。

大概在柔克义抵达美国的时候，他就意识到自己在西藏作了错误的判断。普尔热瓦尔斯基在探险途中病逝后，他的队伍并没有像柔克义预料的那样抵达拉萨，这也意味着自古伯察之后，仍然没有西方人到访过这个雪域圣城。这样一来，柔克义又产生了冲动，他想弥补第一次西藏之旅的缺憾。另一方面，在撰写《喇嘛之地》的过程中，柔克义也发现自己所掌握的材料虽然已经很多，但在某些方面还了解得不够。他"对第一次西藏考察的结果

---

[1] Sven Heiden, *Through Asia,* Vol.1, London: Methuen & Co.,1898, p.11.

并不十分满意"[1]，他想通过第二次考察进一步深入研究。此外，《世纪》杂志的销量以及《喇嘛之地》一书受欢迎的程度显示了从普通读者到政界、学界对他西藏考察的认可和支持，这给了柔克义很大的鼓舞，他下定决心再次前往西藏考察。

1891年10月底柔克义到达上海，这次他吸取了经验教训，为了避免因不能提供官方文件而导致被藏人怀疑，柔克义通过美国史密森学会的帮助从清政府总理衙门取得了特别护照，获得了访问蒙古和青海的权利。

跟第一次西藏之行的时间和路线完全相同，柔克义仍然选择冬季从青海进入西藏。这个时节北方和青藏高原异常寒冷，人们身上御寒的衣物很多，便于乔装改扮。虽然柔克义取得了总理衙门的特别护照，但这只授权他在青海、川康一带访问，进入西藏仍属非法。而他要想深入西藏腹地，就必须偷偷前进，知道的人越少越好。柔克义一行于1891年12月1日离开北京，1892年1月，他抵达兰州。

与第一次考察不同，队伍从青海湖南侧进入柴达木盆地，经过巴隆、格尔木向西南前进，这就是今天青海西藏之间的重要交通线，青藏公路和铁路都无一例外地选择了这条线路。

队伍在三月中旬离开塔尔寺朝着西南方向穿过柴达木盆地向最原始、最荒凉的藏北地区前进。在中亚沙漠中，生命存在很困难。大自然没有任何吸引力，它荒凉无趣。看不到一棵树，也很少有花。可能高原地区的植物群落就是不大发达。

---

[1] William Woodville Rockhill, A Journey in Mongolia and Tibet, *The Geographical Journal*, Vol. III, No.5 (May 1894), p.2.

柔克义在 1892 年 5 月翻过昆仑山进入可可西里，6 月底翻越唐古拉山口进入西藏。在两个月的时间里，他冒着雨雪和冰雹等恶劣天气连续翻越几座大山，成功穿越了无人区。

雨雪冰雹常常把衣服弄湿，……但无论何时，我总是罗盘和笔记本在手，记录周围的环境、走过的距离和地形。一有时间，如果不是太晚，我就写下一天工作的记录。然后还要照顾骡马。

柔克义的队伍在翻过唐古拉山后终于碰到了一些藏民，他们得知方向是对的，而且已经越来越接近拉萨了。沿着道路，柔克义走到了那曲西南纳木错附近的地方。对他来说，碰到人烟，是好事也是坏事。好的是可以得到食物、辨别方向；坏的是行踪很快暴露，各种阻挠也接踵而来。

在纳木错附近，柔克义终于被藏兵发现，他并没有隐瞒身份，如实回答了藏兵的提问——你是谁？为什么来此地？要去哪儿？藏兵们很客气，但是告诉柔克义：你必须原路返回。他们说柔克义根本没有办法翻越那些高山。3 天以后，来了一位级别更高的藏兵军官，他决定派人护卫柔克义出藏，实际上是将其押解出境。在 10 名藏兵的陪同下，柔克义从纳木错附近返回那曲。藏兵把他们送上从那曲向东的大路后就离开了。柔克义知道已无可能再去拉萨，他不得不接受现实，放弃原来的计划，沿着道路从那曲到昌都，再辗转至打箭炉。在路上走了两个多月后，10 月 2 日，他抵达打箭炉，接下来便和 1889 年的路线一模一样，沿着长江顺流而下。10 月底，柔克义到达上海。

柔克义的这次旅行比第一次距离远、时间长，所经地区的自然条件更加恶劣，他翻越的昆仑山和唐古拉山海拔都在六七千米以上，对体力的消耗更大。此外，柔克义再度患上了雪盲症，尽管海上航行有助于他的恢复，但他仍需要照顾和药物治疗。

回到美国的柔克义很快养好了身体重新投入到学术研究中。这次蒙藏考察的成果颇为丰富，最显著的就是他带回了跟西藏文化相关的大量实物以及实地拍摄的许多照片。考察中柔克义总计行程 12874 公里，进行了 3471 次观测，所过山口 69 个，进行了 100 个地理观测点的经纬度测量，拍摄了 300 多张照片，搜集了三四百件民族学物品以及若干地质和动植物标本[1]。

在两年前的那次西藏之行中，柔克义只是测量地形和水文情况、做各种科学记录，并没有留心搜集器物。这一次，史密森学会给柔克义的任务之一就是为旗下的博物馆搜集有关西藏的藏品。由于考察路线途经内蒙古，柔克义也搜集了有关蒙古的物品。史密森学会收购了柔克义带回的全部器物，还聘请他为这些藏品编目、分类，以进行相关研究。柔克义对亲手搜集的这些物品十分熟悉，了解它们的来源、用途和文化含义。他很快为史密森学会撰写出一部长篇报告《西藏人类学笔记》(*Notes on the Ethnology of Tibet*)，发表在 1893 年美国国家博物馆年度报告上。这份长达 82 页的报告，详细介绍了西藏的历史文明、藏人的性格、社会组织、建筑环境、饮食服饰、交通地理、风俗宗教等情况，并附有 52 张图版，将所搜集到的器物与藏人的生活一一对应起来，其中还有不少柔克义在西藏拍摄的实景照片，给读者以最直观的方式来理解西藏的历史、文化和宗教。

---

[1] William Woodville Rockhill, A Journey in Mongolia and in Tibet, *The Geographical Journal*, Vol.3, No.5(May 1894), pp.357-384.

1895 年，这本报告还以单行本的形式再版发行[1]。柔克义所搜集的器物在当时来看大多并不贵重，都是蒙、藏、汉民们日常生活所使用的东西，例如他带回了四川地区最低层民众所穿的草鞋。而以今天的眼光看，这些东西无疑都非常珍贵，它们成为研究历史、民俗、宗教无可替代的宝贵材料。正是这批藏品奠定了史密森学会旗下博物馆的中国收藏基础。柔克义也与史密森学会保持了长久的联系，他在随后的中国任职期间，一直承担着为史密森学会、美国国会图书馆、美国东方学会等机构采购中文图书和文物的工作。

《世纪》杂志在听说柔克义从中国返回后，再一次找到他，希望刊登有关这次蒙藏之旅的文章。柔克义欣然应允，在 1892 年 4 月号的《世纪》杂志上发表了题为《被驱逐出藏》（*Driven out of Tibet*）的文章，介绍了本次蒙藏旅行的大体情形。5 月底，英国皇家地理学会决定授予他金质奖章，以表彰其 1888 年的西藏考察以及《喇嘛之地》一书对地理学的贡献。

1894 年底，柔克义第二次西藏考察的研究著述《1891 和 1892 年蒙藏旅行日记》（*Diary of a Journey through Mongolia and Tibet in 1891 and 1892*）正式出版了。该书由史密森学会而不是一个商业出版社出版，因此书评并没有第一本书那么广泛，但有限的一些书评都给予了高度的评价。这本书同样包含了大量科学考察的数据和地图，对于美国人乃至整个西方世界了解西藏具有重要意义。

---

[1] William Woodville Rockhill, *Notes on the Ethnology of Tibet,* Washington: Government Printing Office, 1895.

　　柔克义的两次西藏考察和相关著述奠定了他在藏学研究领域的地位。他是第一位进入西藏地区的美国人，也是少有的懂藏语的西方人之一。他对西藏宗教、文学、人类学、民俗学和历史的研究具有较高的学术价值。他在考察途中携带现代地理学的测量工具，对西藏地理环境进行科学观测和记录，留下了第一手的科学数据，还将考察路线绘制成精确的地图。对西藏的考察和研究为他后来外交生涯中处理涉藏事务奠定了坚实的学术基础。他后来多次在文章中提出"西藏是中国一部分"的说法，这个结论也是建立在他长期对西藏研究和实地调查基础上的，绝不是随便说说，柔克义在现实和历史文献中都找到了证据。

William W. Rockhill

⑪ "柔克义涉藏档案"的基本情况、历史价值和现实意义

Introduction of Documents Relating to Tibet from Rockhill Papers: Historical Value and Present Significance

柔克义是一位学者型外交官,他在从事外交工作和学术研究的同时,也十分注意保存各种资料和档案,如文章手稿、日记、书信、电报、会谈纪要、报刊剪报和政府文件等。凡是经他手的,且与重大历史事件相关的,他都做了复本备案。

柔克义在 1900 年曾作为总统特使返回中国参加八国联军与清政府的谈判,并代表美国与中国签订了《辛丑条约》;1905 年他再度来华担任美国驻华公使并亲自主持庚子赔款的退款工作;1914 年,他受袁世凯的邀请担任中华民国的外交顾问。他的特殊外交经历使他跟美国以及清政府的很多政要都建立了密切的交往并保持了长期的通信,讨论各种重要问题。这些会谈纪要和书信资料都被柔克义保存下来,成为"柔克义档案"的重要组成部分。

由于柔克义对西藏问题极为关注,又在 1908 年数次与十三世达赖喇嘛会面,达赖喇嘛到北京觐见光绪皇帝和慈禧太后期间,柔克义恰好在北京担任美国驻华公使,他与达赖喇嘛就西藏问题几度通信并会见达赖的特使,更将有关问题以书信的形式向西奥多·罗斯福总统进行了汇报。在处理上述涉藏事务和撰写涉藏文章的过程中,柔克义屡次向美国公众指出"西藏是中国不可分割的一部分",并将这一符合历史和现实的观点介绍给罗斯福总统,更代表美国政府向十三世达赖喇嘛表明了这一立场。因此,这些"涉藏档案"不但具有史料价值,更有极高的现实意义。

一、"柔克义涉藏档案"的基本情况

"柔克义档案"主要保存在美国哈佛大学图书馆，此外，美国国会图书馆、美国国家档案馆等单位也有若干柔克义的信件和著作等。"柔克义涉藏档案"按照类别主要包括如下两个部分：1.有关柔克义西藏旅行的游记和学术研究；2.有关1908年达赖喇嘛到访北京觐见光绪皇帝与慈禧太后的档案文献。有关第1部分的情况，前面在谈到柔克义的藏学研究和西藏游历时已经作了介绍，这里着重说明第2部分"有关1908年达赖喇嘛到访北京觐见光绪皇帝与慈禧太后的档案文献"。

20世纪初，随着清政府的日益衰落，早就对西藏觊觎已久的英国开始蠢蠢欲动，希望在西藏攫取更大的利益。1903年末，日本与俄国的矛盾日益突出，俄国在远东被日本牵制无暇顾及中亚。英国便更加有恃无恐，于1903年12月发动了入侵西藏的战争。在英军占领拉萨之际，十三世达赖喇嘛经青海逃往蒙古，先后在乌兰巴托、山西五台山等地滞留。1905年，柔克义抵达北京担任美国驻华公使，英军入侵西藏也引起了他的关注。流亡中的十三世达赖喇嘛早就听说美国驻华公使柔克义是一位懂藏语的藏学家，还亲自到西藏考察过，希望听听他在西藏事务方面的态度，也希望藉此了解一下美国政府在西藏事务上的立场。1905年，柔克义刚到北京，达赖喇嘛就派人和他建立起联系。

1908年5月，十三世达赖喇嘛再次主动派人到北京与柔克义联系，互通信件并表达了会晤的愿望。1908年6月，柔克义从北京到五台山与达赖喇嘛见面，在19日和21日双方会晤两次。1908年9月28日，十三世达赖喇嘛抵达北京，住在黄寺。10月6日，柔克义前往黄寺与达赖喇嘛再度会晤。10 月 14 日，达赖喇嘛觐见慈禧太后和光绪皇帝，用跪拜的方式传递了非常清晰的信号，即达赖喇嘛是皇帝的臣民，西藏服从中央政府的管辖。10 月 21 日，达赖喇嘛再次派人找到柔克义，就西藏事务征求柔克义的意见。在这次会晤中，柔克义向达赖喇嘛的特使洛桑多吉明确表示：西藏必须服从中央政府，清政府对西藏的各项改革措施，他也表示支持。随后，柔克义将数次与达赖喇嘛及其特使会晤的情况向西奥多·罗斯福总统进行了汇报。由于柔克义是美国藏学研究的第一人，他的观点对美国政府的政策起到了重大影响。1908 年 10 月 30 日，达赖喇嘛接受清政府给予的新封号"诚顺赞化西天大善自在佛"和大量礼物。11 月 3 日，达赖喇嘛参加慈禧太后 75 周岁生日的庆典，并表示祝贺。1908 年年底，慈禧太后和光绪皇帝先后去世，达赖喇嘛又主持了有关的佛教诵经超度仪式。1909 年，他离开北京返回拉萨。

有关 1908 年十三世达赖喇嘛访问北京觐见光绪皇帝和慈禧太后以及柔克义与达赖喇嘛及其特使会晤的情况，柔克义保存了相当丰富的档案资料，这些资料主要包括：

（一）柔克义写给西奥多·罗斯福的两封信件

在信件中，柔克义介绍了他和达赖喇嘛及其特使会晤的情况、会谈的内容等，并将自己对西藏事务的看法和做法向罗斯福总统进行了汇报。

（二）清政府发布的有关达赖喇嘛觐见帝后的圣谕和奏折

柔克义搜集了 1908 年有关达赖喇嘛觐见帝后的圣谕和奏折，这些圣谕和奏折主要刊登在当时的《政府官报》上，柔克义将其翻译成英文，作为美国驻华公使馆的公文发回美国国务院，其中详细记载了达赖喇嘛向光绪皇帝和慈禧太后跪拜的情况。

（三）中文报纸有关达赖喇嘛访问北京的报道

柔克义以剪报的形式搜集了当时中文报纸有关 1908 年达赖喇嘛访问北京的新闻报道，并将其翻译成英文发回美国国务院。这些报纸主要有《中央日报》《顺天时报》等。

（四）英文报纸有关达赖喇嘛访问北京的报道

柔克义以剪报的形式搜集了当时英文报纸有关 1908 年达赖喇嘛访问北京的新闻报道，并将其发回美国国务院。这些报纸主要有《北华捷报》（*North China Daily*）等。

二、"柔克义涉藏档案"的历史价值和现实意义

"柔克义涉藏档案"数量众多，时间跨度较大。由于柔克义特殊的经历和对西藏的研究与游历，其留下来的涉藏档案具有十分珍贵和特殊的历史价值和现实意义。这些材料不但能够以当事人的角度复原历史事实的真相，还可以引发我们对当代西藏问题的思考。特别是他多次在信件和文章中提出"西藏是中国不可分割的一部分"，"西藏必须服从中央政府"以及"达赖喇嘛是皇帝的臣民"等观点对于美国总统西奥多·罗斯福、对于当时的国际社会、对于十三世达赖喇嘛都产生了重要影响。由于柔克义具有"美国驻华公使"的特殊身份和地位，他的观点也代表了 20 世纪初美国的对华政策和在西藏问题上的立场；更由于他是一位"藏学家"和地理探险家，他的结论也不单单是一个外交官的认识，而是建立在历史文献研究和实地调查基础上的结论，经得起学术的检验和推敲。今天读起来，我们仍然能从这些"涉藏档案"中感受到它们重要的历史价值和现实意义。

以下，我选取"柔克义涉藏档案"中的一些具体例子来详细

解读。我将英文原文放在一些重要引文之后，以供对比参考。

（一）柔克义在美国《世纪》杂志上撰文称"西藏是中国不可分割的一部分"

1890 年，柔克义第一次考察西藏返回美国后就开始在《世纪》杂志上连载他的西藏游记。当时很多美国人对于西藏一无所知，就连当时的美国驻华公使田贝（Danby）也不知道西藏究竟在哪里。早在 1886 年，柔克义就曾向田贝请假，打算去西藏考察，但遭到拒绝。田贝竟然许诺柔克义，说他会运用自己在华盛顿的影响力让柔克义担任"驻西藏的公使"。柔克义十分惊讶，问田贝是否知道西藏在哪里，田贝回答说不知道。柔克义在 1890 年出版的《世纪》杂志上详细地记录了这段故事，他写道：

1886 年的一天，我作为美国驻北京公使馆秘书，将一封写给美国国务院的电报交给公使，要求他给予确认支持。我在电报中请求得到 8 个月的无薪休假，以便到中国西部和西藏地区去游历。公使读罢电报，转向我说："我不同意。如果你不在使馆，我得找人代替你干活。不过，我告诉你我会怎么做。既然你这么想去西藏，我会用我在华盛顿的影响力，让他们任命你为那里的常驻公使和总领事。"我怯怯地问他是否知道西藏在什么地方。"不知道"，他回答说，"但这又有什么关系？我会按我说的去做。"

还有什么例证比这更能说明我们对于西藏的无知？这位美国驻华公使竟然不知道西藏正是他被派遣驻扎的这个帝国不可分割的一部分！看到不可能既保住公使馆的职位又实现我多年的探险夙愿，我于是辞去公职，并在 1888 年下半年准备好了旅行，要经过华北、青海湖和柴达木盆地，再从那里到什么地方去……但肯定是西藏的一部分了，只要有人居住的地方，哪里都没有关系，那里一定未被探知又充满乐趣[1]。

（One day in 1886, while I was secretary of the United States Legation at Peking, I took to the minister a dispatch for the Secretary of State, requesting him to indorse it favorably. It was to ask for an eight months' leave of absence, without pay, to travel in Western China and Tibet. The minister read it over, and turning to me said: "I cannot give my approval to this. If you absent yourself from the legation I must have someone to take your place and do your work. But I tell you what I will do: since you are so anxious to see Tibet, I will use all my influence at Washington to have you appointed minister resident and consul-general there." I timidly asked him if he knew where Tibet was. "No," he answered; "but it makes no difference. I'll do what I said." What better illustration could I give of the ignorance in which we are concerning Tibet?

The minister of the United States to China did not know that it was an integral part of the empire to the court of which he was accredited! Seeing that there was no possibility of my retaining my connection with our legation and accomplishing the work of exploration on which I had set my heart years ago, I resigned my post, and in the latter part of 1888 was ready for the journey which would take me through Northern China, the Koko-nor and Ts'aidam countries, and thence whitherward... but certainly into some part of Tibet; and so long as it was an inhabited one, it mattered little: it would be unexplored, and

---

[1] William W. Rockhill, An American in Tibet, *Century Magazine*, Vol. XLI (Nov. 1890), No.1, pp. 4-17.

could not fail to prove interesting.）

柔克义在《世纪》杂志上发表的文章是美国最早介绍西藏的文字之一，《世纪》是当时美国的畅销杂志，发行量极大，影响深远。柔克义在文中清楚地写道"西藏是中国不可分割的一部分"，这对于当时的美国人认识西藏的历史和法律地位起到了至关重要的作用。

（二）柔克义在给西奥多·罗斯福总统的信中写道，"达赖喇嘛作为世俗领袖，必须服从中国中央政府"。他在与达赖喇嘛特使会面时说，"西藏的军事、外交和教育应由中央负责"，"达赖喇嘛必须服从其君主的命令"

在柔克义"涉藏档案"中有两封 1908 年他写给西奥多·罗斯福总统的信件，这两封信集中展示了柔克义与达赖喇嘛及其特使会面的情况和谈话记录，也比较集中地反映了柔克义在西藏事务上的看法。

1908 年 6 月 30 日柔克义给西奥多·罗斯福总统写去了第一封信，汇报他与流亡中的达赖喇嘛的交往情况。他在信中写道：

1905 年我刚刚抵达北京不久，达赖喇嘛便向北京派来两名高级喇嘛作为他的代表，随时向他报告情况以便他相应地安排自己的行动。达赖喇嘛让他们给我捎来一封信和一些礼物，说他听闻我曾到西藏旅行过，学过藏语并读过藏文文献。他料想我会对他的代表持友好态度，并希望我告诉他们他现在该如何是好——是马上返回西藏，还是等英国人全部撤离之后再回去。

1908 年 5 月，达赖喇嘛的一名代表又一次找到柔克义，再度捎来信件和礼物。由于达赖喇嘛此时在五台山居住，距离北京不远，柔克义提议前往会晤以表示感谢，并很快得到达赖喇嘛的同意。

1908 年 6 月 13 日柔克义从北京启程前往山西五台山，19 日和 21 日，他在五台山两次与十三世达赖喇嘛会晤。他在给罗斯福总统的信中详细描写了会晤的情况，包括达赖喇嘛的衣着、容貌、谈吐等。双方讨论的话题主要与西藏有关，达赖喇嘛向柔克义表示"去北京面圣是一件好事，但他尚不知道是否会去"。达赖喇嘛听说柔克义担任驻华公使，希望与他保持通信，以便随时咨询相关事务。柔克义在给罗斯福总统的信中写道：

我告诉他说，我非常荣幸，但因在北京有公务在身，也请他理解我会受到很多限制，仅能在有限的方面为他提供帮助。

在我们的会谈中，达赖喇嘛表示由于西藏地处偏远，没有多少外国的朋友。我说他错了，在美国和其他国家有很多人为他和西藏祈福，希望他和他的人民繁荣幸福。

西奥多·罗斯福总统在 1908 年 9 月就给柔克义回信，表示他十分关心"达赖喇嘛在北京停留期间与清中央政府的交往"，柔克义因此迟至 11 月 8 日才回了第二封信，为的就是能够将十三世达赖喇嘛在北京的全部情况向罗斯福总统作一完整汇报。

1908 年 9 月下旬，达赖喇嘛离开五台山启程前往北京。他经山西太原抵达定州，转乘火车于 9 月 28 日到达北京前门车站。随后，他被安置在北京北郊的藏传佛教寺庙黄寺。

达赖喇嘛抵达北京的第二天即派人前往柔克义处，邀请柔克义率美国公使馆的全体成员访问黄寺。柔克义认为，与达赖的会晤还是应该安排在他觐见慈禧和光绪之后。但由于觐见的日期一再推迟，加之达赖喇嘛再三要求，10月6日，柔克义前往黄寺与达赖喇嘛会面，这是二人自6月在五台山相见以来的第二次会晤。在十分钟的时间里，双方互致问候，柔克义还转达了罗斯福总统对达赖喇嘛馈赠礼物的感谢，达赖则表示一两天后还会派助手回访柔克义。10月14日，达赖喇嘛在颐和园仁寿殿觐见慈禧太后和光绪皇帝，行跪拜礼。10月19日起，达赖喇嘛获得清政府外务部批准，可于每日中午至下午3时接见外国使节。

据柔克义给罗斯福总统的信中记载：10月19日，俄国驻华公使廓索维慈（Korostovetz）转告柔克义，达赖喇嘛的特使洛桑多吉已经拜访了他，咨询有关清政府在西藏推行改革一事，并就达赖喇嘛应留在北京与清政府商谈藏务还是应该立即返回拉萨征求他的意见。廓索维慈告诉洛桑多吉，**"达赖喇嘛应该服从清政府的决定，除此以外他别无建议"**。（Mr. Korostovetz said he had told Dorjieff that he thought the Dalai Lama had only to submit to what the Chinese Government might decide upon, but he had no advice to give.）对于俄国的态度，柔克义向罗斯福总统作了说明：

"作为精神领袖的达赖喇嘛，俄国人对他的福祉倍感兴趣，但作为世俗领袖，他就必须服从中国中央政府。"（The time when Russian was concerned in advising or supporting eastern rulers was at an end; as a spiritual ruler Russian was greatly interested in the welfare of the Dalai Lama, as a temporal ruler he must obey China.）

洛桑多吉则告诉俄国公使廓索维慈，如果达赖喇嘛在俄国人那里得不到什么建议，他就转向英国驻华公使朱尔典去寻求

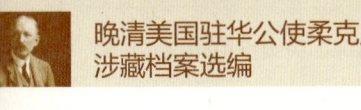

帮助。廓索维慈认为这同样无济于事，因为朱尔典公使已经告诉他说，**"他不能与藏人直接联系，据他所知，涉及西藏的问题应和中国政府商议解决"**。（He could hold no direct relations with the Tibetans; so far as he was concerned, questions concerning Tibet must be settled with the Chinese Government.）廓索维慈建议洛桑多吉去找柔克义，听听与西藏没有任何直接利害关系的美国如何看待此事。

10月21日，洛桑多吉与柔克义会面。他告诉柔克义，达赖喇嘛听说清政府要对西藏行政进行重大改革，但尚不清楚改革的实质和程度。他征求柔克义的意见，达赖应该在北京等到改革内容公布还是应该即刻返回拉萨。因为达赖喇嘛十分担心一旦改革内容敲定，他以及前代达赖喇嘛的权利就会被清政府削减。柔克义则回答说：

> 我从中国的新闻报纸上了解到清政府正在酝酿有关西藏的行政改革，包括将西藏划分为与中国内地相同的行政区划，重新组建西藏的军事力量，改革财政、教育，发展农牧业以及修建道路等。如果这真是计划中的改革内容，我看不到达赖喇嘛反对这项改革的任何理由。不仅如此，军事、外交和教育问题（在某些地区）都是皇家中央的分内之事，不应该留给各个省份去单独处理。

> （I understood from the Chinese public press that the Government contemplated an administrative reform of Tibet, the dividing of the country into regular administrative districts as in China proper, the reorganization of the military forces of the country, of the currency, of education, the extension or agriculture and stock-raising, and of the opening of roads, etc. If these were really the reforms

contemplated, I could not see what objection the Dalai Lama could have to them. Furthermore, military questions, relations with foreign states, educational questions (in some countries) were all imperial matters which could not be left to the various states to deal with independently.）

洛桑多吉说，"达赖喇嘛绝不反对在西藏发展教育或进行军事改革"，他只有两点要求：一是黄教应继续保持其在西藏的声誉，二是达赖本人有直接向皇帝上书言事的权利。柔克义则表示：

我确信，皇帝和他的政府绝不会做任何贬低黄教声誉的事，这也是该王朝一贯所持的传统政策。……我认为他（指达赖喇嘛）很可能满怀信心地指望能继续获得帝国的支持。关于第二点，我建议达赖喇嘛非正式地了解一下，这样的要求怎样才能被转递到皇帝手中并被恰当处理。我个人认为他的要求是合理的，对于政府的良好运作也是有益的，可以保证他的代表能直接与皇帝接触。如果清政府意识到达赖喇嘛对于这项特权是多么渴望，我认为他们不会严重反对此事。

（I felt convinced that the Emperor and His Government would do nothing whatsoever to lessen the dignity of the Yellow Church, that it was the traditional policy of his dynasty to uphold it; I thought he might confidently count on a continuance of the Imperial Favor. Concerning the second point, I advised the Dalai Lama to ascertain informally how such a request would be received and act accordingly. Personally I thought what he asked for was reasonable and in the interest of good government, that it insured his representations reaching the Throne and that I could not see what serious objections could be made to it if the Chinese Government was made aware how greatly he desired this privileges.）

关于达赖喇嘛去留北京的问题，洛桑多吉表示只要上述两项要求得到确认，达赖喇嘛将立即返回拉萨，其他事情由留在北京的堪布喇嘛与理藩部协商处理。对此，柔克义有不同的意见，他说：

过去三年来，我一直建议达赖喇嘛尽早返回拉萨，勿要迟疑。现在我仍然认为这是上策。然而，他应向中国政府表明，他本人是发自内心地支持（清廷）在西藏采取的各项利于西藏的举措，因为他能否继续得到清廷的支持，以及清廷是否能给予他所期望的支持，完全取决于此。

(I said that I had for the last three years constantly advised the Dalai Lama to return without delay to Lhasa, and that I still thought this highly desirable. He should, however, show the Chinese Government that he was sincerely favorable to all measures for the good of his country, as on this must depend the continuance of the Imperial favor and the granting to him of the favors he so much desired.)

俄、英、美三国公使的态度，特别是柔克义与洛桑多吉的长谈让达赖喇嘛打消了疑虑和立即返回拉萨的念头，留在北京参加各种礼仪活动和有关藏务改革的磋商。也正是因此，达赖喇嘛才赶上了慈禧太后的生日以及慈禧和光绪皇帝去世，他随后主持了超度诵经的活动。

通过与洛桑多吉的谈话，柔克义了解了达赖喇嘛的诉求，他在给罗斯福总统的信中指出：

从这次长时间的谈话，我得出（如下）结论：凡不影响他个人特权的事情，他几乎都不会在意；他将自己的事业与西藏人民的事业区分得泾渭分明，他愿意将西藏人民的事业完全交由清廷任意处置。只要他觉得他的个人荣誉和特权能有所保障，如有可能还可增加的话，他就不会特别在意（清廷）打算在西藏进行的行政改革。清政府一定也得出了同样的结论。虽然清廷仅仅将他视作黄教首领，也予以他相应的尊重，但这都让他清楚地意识到：他是皇帝的臣民。

(I gathered from this very long conversation that the Dalai Lama cared very little, if at all, for anything which did not affect his personal privileges and prerogatives, that he separated entirely his cause from that of the people of Tibet, which he was willing to abandon entirely to the mercy of China. He did not care particularly concerning the contemplated administrative reforms, so long as he could feel assured that his personal honors and privileges were safe and, if possible, slightly added to. The Chinese Government must have reached the same conclusion. While it has treated him simply as the head of the Yellow Church and has shown him honors accordingly, it has made him clearly realized the he was a Subject of the Emperor.)

事实也正如柔克义预料的那样，清政府秉承了一贯的支持黄教的做法，但在奏事方面，达赖喇嘛则要按照惯例，将奏折交给驻藏大臣代为转奏。11 月 3 日，达赖喇嘛又一次派人来找柔克义，就"由驻藏大臣转递奏折"的问题再来咨询。柔克义回答说：

看起来没有办法解决这个难题，达赖喇嘛必须服从其君主的命令，他已经得到了很多荣誉封号，与印度的关系也得到了清政府的满意安排，黄教的利益也得以保全。在得到好处的同时也必须作出让步。我对他唯一的建议，就是不要再犹豫迟疑，立即答应清政府的要求，否则将引起误解并导致事态进一步趋向复杂。

(I said that I saw absolutely no way out of the difficulty; the Dalai Lama must submit to his sovereign's command. He had received many honors, his relations with India had been satisfactorily arranged by China, the interests of the Yellow Church were safe. He must take the bitter with the sweet, and the only suggestion I could make that he should not delay too long complying with the wishes of the Chinese Government, as it might be misunderstood and lead to further complications.)

柔克义随后将他与洛桑多吉的谈话内容转告了俄国驻华公使廓索维慈和英国驻华公使朱尔典，并且相信他们对自己的观点均无异议。

在与达赖喇嘛特使会面的过程中，柔克义把自己对西藏问题的态度清晰且明白无误地传递给达赖喇嘛，即他认为"西藏是中国不可分割的一部分，应该服从中央政府管辖；达赖喇嘛是皇帝的臣民，必须服从君主的命令"，对于清政府可能实行的西藏改革计划，柔克义持赞成态度，并希望达赖喇嘛也表示支持。柔克义在给西奥多·罗斯福总统的信中也提到了当时的俄国公使廓索维慈和英国公使朱尔典对西藏事务的态度，他们也都公开表示，"达赖喇嘛应该服从清政府的决定"，"作为世俗领袖，他必须服从中国中央政府"，"西藏问题应由中国政府解决"等。上述表述清楚地表明，20 世纪初期，不仅仅是美国，即使是想在西藏攫取更大利益的英国和俄国，也公开承认"西藏是中国领土，中国中央政府对西藏拥有主权"。

（三）柔克义所搜集的"有关达赖喇嘛觐见光绪皇帝和慈禧太后"的剪报、奏折及其发回美国国务院的翻译向美国政府表明：达赖喇嘛在觐见时以"跪拜"的礼节表示其臣服于中央政府

1908 年，当十三世达赖喇嘛访问北京时，当时的西方驻华外交官虽然可以拜访暂居在黄寺的达赖喇嘛，但他们未能参加达赖喇嘛与慈禧、光绪的会面仪式，对于各方面的具体细节了解不多。而当时清政府颁发的各种谕旨和理藩部大臣的奏折则详细记载了达赖喇嘛陛见帝后的全过程，其中相当一部分在当时出版的《政治官报》中得到披露。此外，全国各地的报纸，如《中央日报》《顺天时报》等也对达赖喇嘛访问北京作了详细的报道。但受到语言的限制，多数外交官并不能从《政府官报》以及中文报纸中得到太大的帮助。而柔克义却与众不同，他良好的汉语水平使他从上述材料中获得了大量有用信息。他不但搜集了相关的谕旨、奏折和新闻报道，而且将这些内容及时地翻译成英文报告给当时的美国政府，使美国政府对于当时达赖喇嘛用跪拜礼表示臣服于中央政府的态度得以非常清楚地了解。从现在的角度看，这些材料年代久远又较为分散，而柔克义能够将其较为完整地搜集起来是难能可贵的。

今天，这些一百多年前的报纸已不易找到，十分珍贵。此外，这些文献中还引用了很多当时发布的上谕和奏折，其中很多已经散佚，这更加凸显了这些档案的价值。例如，其中《达赖喇嘛陛见礼节》一文对于达赖与慈禧及光绪见面和跪拜的情况记载尤为详细，由中国第一历史档案馆和中国藏学研究中心根据清宫档案编撰的《清末十三世达赖喇嘛档案史料选编》（中国藏学出版社2002年版）一书中也未有如此详细的记载，足见柔克义档案的珍贵。这则档案的内容如下：

达赖喇嘛陛见礼节

　　九月廿日达赖喇嘛觐见两宫礼节见录如左：是日，皇太后升仁寿殿，召御前大臣并御前侍卫等至仁寿殿内侍立，理藩部堂官分引达赖喇嘛并通事喇嘛二名、堪布喇嘛四名进仁寿殿左门，由纳陛左阶引达赖喇嘛纳陛上侧跪，通事喇嘛二名跪于达赖喇嘛之次，堪布喇嘛四名于纳陛下侧跪。达赖喇嘛敬谨跪递佛一尊、哈达一方，御前大臣接受。堪布喇嘛四名于原跪处敬谨跪递哈达，御前侍卫接受。达赖喇嘛跪请皇太后圣安，叩谢恩赏，跪听皇太后宣谕。达赖喇嘛奏对仍由通事喇嘛递相转答。御前大臣覆"奏礼毕"，引出恭候。皇上升仁寿殿，理藩部堂官分引达赖喇嘛并通事喇嘛二名、堪布喇嘛四名进仁寿殿右门，达赖喇嘛敬谨跪递佛一尊、哈达一方；理藩部堂官引通事喇嘛二名、堪布喇嘛四名均跪于达赖喇嘛之后。堪布喇嘛四名敬谨跪递哈达，御前侍卫接受。达赖喇嘛恭请圣安，叩谢恩赏。理藩部堂官引通事喇嘛跪于达赖喇嘛之次，堪布喇嘛四名跪于达赖喇嘛之后，跪听皇上宣谕。达赖喇嘛奏对仍由通事喇嘛递相转达。御前大臣覆"奏毕礼毕"，引出。

Ceremony at the Audience granted to the Dalai Lama

　　On the 20th, of the Ninth Moon (Oct.14th, 1908) the Dalai Lama will have audience of Their Imperial Majesties, the Empress Dowager and the Emperor. The ceremony will be as follows:

On the day stated H.I.M. the Empress Dowager will ascend the throne in the Jen Shou Tien and will summon the Ministers of the Presence, as well as the commands of the Imperial Body Guard, to the Jen Shou Tien, to be in attendance upon the officers of the Ministry of Dependencies, who will introduce the Dalai Lama together with the two lama interpreters and the four lama abbots. They will lead them into the Jen Shou Tien through the eastern opening of the doorway. The Master of Ceremonies will then ascend the throne dais with the Dalai Lama, going up by the eastern steps. The Master of Ceremonies will then step to one side and kneel. The two lama interpreters and the four lama abbots will also kneel beside and below the Master of Ceremonies[1].

The Dalai Lama will reverently and respectfully kneel and present a Buddhist image and a scarf. The Minister of the Presence will receive them. The four abbots will pay their reverence in the place where they are kneeling, and will present scarfs. The Commander of the Body Guard will receive them.

The Dalai Lama, kneeling, will express a wish for the health of H.I.M. the Empress Dowager and will kotow as a manifestation of his gratitude to her for the favor shown in bestowing the audience.

The two lama interpreters will translate the commands of the Empress Dowager to the Dalai Lama and his responses to the Throne.

The Minister of the Presence will then request that the audience be closed, and will conduct the guests out of the audience chamber to await

---

[1] 柔克义错误地理解了原文"纳陛"的含义，将其误译为"Master of Ceremonies"。

reverently the entrance to the Jen Shou Tien of H.I.M. the Emperor.

The officers of the Ministry of Dependencies will separately lead into the Jen Shou Tien the Dalai Lama, the two lama interpreters and the four abbots. They will go in by the western opening of the doorway. The Dalai Lama will reverently and respectfully kneel and present to His Majesty a Buddhist image and a scarf. The officers of the Ministry of Dependencies, conducting the two lama interpreters and the four abbots, will cause them to kneel behind the Dalai Lama. The four abbots, while kneeling, will reverently present their scarfs, which the Commander of the Body Guard will receive.

The Dalai Lama will ask after the health of H.I.M. the emperor and kotow to him as an expression of his thankfulness for the favor of the audience. The officers of the Ministry of Dependencies will bring the two lama interpreters close to the Dalai Lama. The four abbots will continue kneeling behind the Dalai Lama. All will reverently listen to his Majesty's commands, to which the Dalai Lama will reply. The two lama interpreters will translate the conversation. After this the Minister of the Presence will request that the audience be closed, and will conduct the visitors to the outside.

这些材料被柔克义译成英文，并以官方文件的形式发给美国国务院，使美国政府第一时间了解了十三世达赖喇嘛觐见慈禧太后和光绪皇帝的情形，以及他通过跪拜的形式所表达的臣服中央政府的政治态度。这些文献对于美国政府在 19 世纪末和 20 世纪初制定对华政策，特别是涉藏事务产生了深远影响。

除了有关达赖喇嘛陛见帝后的情况外，柔克义还保存了很多当时清政府筹划西藏政务改革的资料等。

　　当然，囿于汉语水平的限制，柔克义的翻译也有出现错误的情况。但总体来看，这些误译数量不多，也不影响文献的整体准确性。

　　柔克义涉藏档案数量丰富，内容广泛，其中很多都是其他档案文献中所没有的，从特殊的角度记录了西藏在晚清时期的历史发展。加之柔克义与十三世达赖喇嘛相识，又以美国驻华公使的身份见证了 1908 年十三世达赖喇嘛访问北京觐见光绪和慈禧的过程，他所保留的各种涉藏文献价值十分突出。更为难能可贵的是，柔克义从历史和现实出发，实事求是地对西藏的历史和法律地位作出了正确的判断。他坚持"西藏是中国不可分割的一部分"，"达赖喇嘛应服从中央政府"等观点，向美国政府和西奥多·罗斯福总统提供了正确的信息以形成美国的对华政策，也向十三世达赖喇嘛本人乃至国际社会清晰传递了美国政府的立场，这就使他的涉藏档案具有了很大的现实意义。当然，柔克义作为美国的政府官员，在提出和推行上述涉藏观点时，仍然是以维护美国国家利益为目的，但不得不承认，柔克义是在研究和调查之后得出了正确结论，而这个结论也符合美国的在华利益。

　　此外，我们也必须看到，柔克义是一个学者型的官员，他对学术研究投入了大量的精力，对于他研究的对象——中国，他也投入了很大的情感。柔克义自己曾说：**"西藏是我一生的挚爱"**（Tibet has been my life hobby），连西奥多·罗斯福总统的女儿在提到柔克义时，也在日记中写道：**"中国已经融入了他的血液"**（China has gotten into his blood）。无论从历史还是现实角度来看，柔克义"涉藏档案"都具有很高的研究价值。

William W. Rockhill

Ⅲ 柔克义涉藏档案选编

Selected Documents Relating to Tibet from Rockhill Papers

一、柔克义关于西藏旅行的游记和学术研究

AN AMERICAN IN TIBET[1]
AN ACCOUNT OF A JOURNEY THROUGH AN UNKNOWN LAND
美国人在西藏 [2]
探索未知领域的神奇之旅

AUTHOR'S PREFACE
作者前言

A learned French missionary who for thirty years has been living on the Tibetan borderland, writing some years ago of Tibet, said:

很多年前，一位学识丰富的法国使节曾在西藏边境生活了三十载。在他笔下，西藏是这样的：

What is known of the great plateau which stretches out from the valley of the Tsang-po to the Kuenlun range? The same may be asked of the form of government, the civil and military organization, the rights of ownership, the civil and religious condition of the people, their virtues and vices, their morals and their customs. Who can speak of the geology, the mineralogy, the mines of Tibet? What is the value of its commerce, both domestic and foreign?

广袤的西藏高原从雅鲁藏布江河谷绵延数千里一直到巍峨的昆仑山脉。关于这片高原，人们都知道什么呢？关于西藏的政体形式、民

---

[1]　William W. Rockhill, An American in Tibet, *Century Magazine,* Vol. XLI (Nov. 1890), No.1, pp. 3-4

[2]　威廉·柔克义，《美国人在西藏》，《世纪杂志》，第四十一卷（1890 年 11 月），第 1 期，第 3—4 页。

间与军事组织、所有权、当地人的民间生存状态和宗教信仰、当地人的人性善恶、道德面貌与风俗习惯，人们又都知道什么呢？谁能述说西藏的地质、矿物和矿藏呢？西藏的商业对于中国和国外分别具有什么样的价值呢？

Instead of applying themselves to throw some light on these and many other questions, people generally, and even savants, have only this to say: Tibet is the poorest country in the world; it has nothing to sell, there is nothing to be gotten out of it. A convenient answer, in truth, but one which only proves that Tibet is a perfect terra incognita. A big volume might be written on what we do not know about Tibet; and if such a book was ever written and had the good fortune to be read, it would dispel many of our illusions.

不过，一般来说，人们甚至就连学者们也并没有致力于阐明这些问题。除此之外，还有很多其他问题。他们只是轻描淡写地说：西藏是世界上最穷的地区；当地没有什么物产，也没什么物品可以外销。确实，做出这个回答似乎很便利，但这也只是证明：西藏确实是一片神奇的未知土地。关于我们所不知道的西藏"面面观"，可以撰写一部大部头。真要是能写出这样一部书，真要是有幸有人来读，那么说不定就能消散我们关于这片土地的所有幻觉。

Thus said Abbé Desgodins in 1881, and ten years have added but little to our knowledge. Of the many attempts made within the last fifty years to penetrate Tibet none have been really successful save that of Hue in 1845, whose charming work has but little scientific or geographical value. Other travelers have gone as far as Bat'ang, on the high road between China and Lh'asa, but have invariably been stopped at that point. Prjevalsky's explorations never extended to Tibet proper, unless we apply that name to the desert and uninhabitable tablelands on the north of that country.

1881 年，德格丹神父就是这样说的。十年过去了，但我们对于西藏的了解似乎一点都没有增加。在过去的五十年中，人们做了很多尝试来深入西藏腹地，但都没有取得实质的成功。只有一个例外，那就是法国传教士古伯察（Evariste Régis Huc）在 1845 年的壮举。不过，虽然他的探险令人陶醉，但却没什么科学或地理方面的价值。一些旅行者最远曾抵达了位于进藏路上的巴塘县，但随后便无一例外地被天堑阻隔，无法继续前行。尼古拉·米哈伊洛维奇·普尔热瓦尔斯基以远征中亚和东亚闻名，不过就连他也从未真正到过西藏本土，而只是曾经踏上了西藏北部那片广袤的沙漠和荒无人烟的高原。

In northeastern Tibet foreign travelers had not been more successful. In 1884-85 Colonel Prjevalsky, with an escort of fourteen Cossacks and sixty-five camels, was unable to enter it, and a few years previously Count Szechenyi and his expedition had not been allowed by the Chinese authorities to advance in this direction.

在西藏东北部，各国的旅行者们也没能成功。1884 至 1885 年间，在十四个哥萨克人驾着六十五匹骆驼的护送下，普尔热瓦尔斯基上校也没能进入西藏。而在此前的几年，中国当局根本都不允许赛切尼伯爵和远征队朝那一方向挺进。

Of the great value of exploration in this part of the country it may be noted that Prjevalsky in his last work speaks of it as among the *spolia opima* of future travelers, and it is said that Stanley was so alive to it that he expressed at one time a strong desire to attempt a journey there.

说起这一地区远征活动的巨大价值，我们应该指出，在最后的著作中，普尔热瓦尔斯基曾将西藏称为后世探险家们的"至尊战利品"。据说，斯坦利也充分意识到了这一点。他有次就曾表达了进藏探险的强烈愿望。

Besides the attraction which travelers would naturally feel for an entirely unexplored region, this one was known, from Chinese sources, to present many features of peculiar interest.

作为一处完全未被发掘的处女地，西藏的魅力自然吸引着来自世界各地的旅行家和探险家。不过除此之外，从汉语资料来看，西藏有着颇多特点，别有一番意趣。

A primitive political organization; nomadic tribes, among them the Golok, the most lawless and most feared throughout the country; old and quaint customs which had disappeared from the more civilized parts of Tibet—all pointed to it as showing Tibetan culture in its early and primitive form. It was said to be a well-watered land, traversed by a number of important rivers, presenting many varieties of climate and vegetation, rich in mineral wealth, and the habitat of a great variety of wild animals, many of them unknown to naturalists.

一种原始的政治组织；游牧部落，其中包括西藏最目无法纪、最令人闻风丧胆的果洛人；在西藏文明较为开化的地区已经消失的古老而有趣的风俗习惯——所有这些都指向着早期的原始西藏文化。据称，在过去西藏曾是一片水量充沛的富饶之地，多条重要河流在此汇聚，气候多变，草木植被浓郁葱茏，矿物资源丰富，是大量野生动物栖息的乐土。这些野生动物有很多就连自然学家们都叫不上名字来。

For years I had wished to visit Tibet, especially this part of it. From the time I was a boy I was much interested in Tibetan Buddhism, and I early acquired a fairly good knowledge of the literary language. So when, in 1884, I was attached to the United States Legation in Peking, it seemed as though I might be able to carry out my plans of exploration if I could learn the spoken language, a knowledge of which, from the first, I held to be an absolute requisite for success. No foreigner spoke the language, and none of the natives whom I first met would consent to teach me, being suspicious of the use I might make of my learning. I finally gained the friendship of an intelligent Lama from Lh'asa, and with him for the next four years I studied Tibetan, giving also much of my time to the study of Chinese.

多年来，我一直梦想着去西藏旅行，特别想去西藏的这一地区。我自小就对藏传佛教颇感兴趣，而且很早我就较为娴熟地掌握了文学语言（书面语）。因此，到了 1884 年开始在驻北京美国公使馆工作时，我就想，要是能学会口语，也许自己长期以来去西藏探险的夙愿就能实现了。我从一开始就认为，娴熟的口语水平是成功进藏的必要条件。没有外国人会讲这种语言，而且我一开始见到的那些当地人也都不愿意教我，因为他们很怀疑我的学习目的。不过最后，我还是和拉萨一位聪明的喇嘛建立了友谊。在接下来的四年里，我孜孜不倦地向他学习藏语，还花了大量时间学习汉语。

In the autumn of 1888, having resigned my position in the diplomatic service, I started on my travels to this strange land.

1888 年秋天，我辞去外交职位，开始向这片神奇的土地进发。

My whole journey from Peking through Tibet to Shanghai occupied nine months. From where I left the Ts'aidam till I reached Ta-chien-lu had never before been trodden by a white man. All this country I was able to survey, besides correcting some errors of previous travelers in the Koko-nor and Ts'aidam, and adding something to our knowledge of those little-known regions.

我此次旅行的起点是北京，目的地是西藏，之后再返回上海。整个旅程历时九个月。从我离开柴达木盆地，直到最终到达打箭炉镇（现在的康定市行政区域所在地，过去被称为"打箭炉"，或简称"炉城"），从来没有白人踏上过这片土地。此次跨越西藏全境的旅行让我受益匪浅，我仔细勘察、纠正曾去过青海湖和柴达木盆地的那些前辈旅行者们的一些错误，也加上了一些信息，让大家更加了解这片我们知之甚少的土地。

THROUGH NORTHERN CHINA TO THE KOKO-NOR[1]
从中国北方到青海湖 [2]

One day in 1886, while I was secretary of the United States Legation at Peking, I took to the minister a dispatch for the Secretary of State, requesting him to indorse it favorably. It was to ask for an eight months' leave of absence, without pay, to travel in Western China and Tibet. The minister read it over, and turning to me said: "I cannot give my approval to this. If you absent yourself from the legation I must have someone to take your place and do your work. But I tell you what I will do: since you are so anxious to see Tibet, I will use all my influence at Washington to have you appointed minister resident and consul-general there." I timidly asked him if he knew where Tibet was. "No," he answered; "but it makes no difference. I'll do what I said."

时间回到 1886 年的一天，当时我还是美国驻北京公使馆秘书。我拿着急件，去找公使，希望他上呈国务卿。上面我用恳切的语气，请求他签字同意我无薪休假八个月，去中国西部和西藏游历。公使读完信，对我说："抱歉，我不能同意。要是你不在公使馆工作，我得找人代替你，工作总得做啊。不过话说回来，我能帮你个忙。既然你那么想去西藏看看，我可以动用华盛顿的关系，任命你做那儿的常驻公使兼总领事。"我大着胆子问他是否知道西藏在哪里。他回答："我不知道，不过这没什么大不了的，我说话算话。"

What better illustration could I give of the ignorance in which we are concerning Tibet?

---

[1]　William W. Rockhill, An American in Tibet, *The Century*, Vol. XLI (Nov. 1890), No.1, pp. 4-17.

[2]　威廉·柔克义，《美国人在西藏》，《世纪杂志》，第四十一卷（1890 年 11 月），第 1 期，第 4—17 页。

看到了吧？难道我还需要进一步阐述人们对西藏的了解有多么匮乏吗？

The minister of the United States to China did not know that it was an integral part of the empire to the court of which he was accredited! Seeing that there was no possibility of my retaining my connection with our legation and accomplishing the work of exploration on which I had set my heart years ago, I resigned my post, and in the latter part of 1888 was ready for the journey which would take me through Northern China, the Koko-nor and Ts'aidam countries, and thence whitherward, as Carlyle would say, but certainly into some part of Tibet; and so long as it was an inhabited one, it mattered little: it would be unexplored, and could not fail to prove interesting.

就连美国驻中国公使都不知道西藏是他受命服务的那个庞大帝国不可分割的一部分领土！唉！看到不可能既保住公使馆的职位，又实现我多年进藏探险的夙愿，我最终辞去了工作。1888 年下半年，我收拾好行装，准备向中国北方进发，穿过那里，最终抵达青海湖和柴达木盆地。然后，就像卡莱尔说的那样，从那里一直朝着西藏的方向前进，当然最终要抵达某些藏区。无论是哪里都没有关系，只要有人居住就行。而那片没有开发过的处女地，是绝不会让我失望的。

Travel in Northern China is accomplished in a cart, a mule litter, or the saddle.

在中国北方旅行，我要么得乘坐二轮马车，要么得乘坐骡子拉的轿子，要么就得骑马。

The first method is the most uncomfortable but the most rapid, the second the most comfortable but the slowest, the third the most independent but the most uncertain. The cart used in Northern China has two heavy wheels, with wooden axle, no springs, and a body about four feet long and three broad, over which is a light framework top covered with blue cotton. Two mules driven tandem by a carter seated on the left shaft take it along at a rate of about three miles an hour, and one can make in it an average of thirty-five miles a day, even over the roughest country. It will carry about three hundred pounds of goods, and one or even two passengers; and the tighter one is squeezed in the more comfortable it will prove, for that, and that alone, will be a protection from the terrible jolting over the rough country roads.

第一个选择最不舒服，但最快。第二个选择最舒服，但最慢。第三种选择最自由，但不那么靠谱。中国北方使用的马车装有两个重重的轮子，车轴是木制的，没有弹簧。整个车身大约四英尺长，三英尺宽。上部装有很轻的车架顶棚，蒙着蓝色的棉布。驾车人坐在左侧的主轴上，驾着纵向排列的两头骡子，以大约每小时三英里的速度行进。乘坐这种交通工具，每人每天平均可以走三十五英里。即使在最颠簸的乡村道路上，速度也差不多。这种马车还大约可以负载三百磅物品，一两位乘客。马车的空间越拥挤，事实证明乘客就越舒服。因为，也只有这一点才能让人们在崎岖不平的乡村道路上，免受颠簸之苦。

It is told in some old book of travel, in the narrative of the mission of Lord Amherst to the court of Peking, if I remember rightly, that one of his attendants died from the effects of the jolting he received during a short journey in one of these carts. But this mode of travel being the most rapid, I adopted it. Several years of experience of cart travel in China had made me bold, so that I did not fear the fate which had overtaken the Amherst mission man. Comfortably wrapped in my wadded Chinese clothes, I squeezed myself into my cart, feeling like a delicate piece of china ware packed in cotton, and after a hearty farewell to the friends with whom I was staying at Peking, the carters cracked their whips, and with a shout to the mules we were off.

过去的一些游记曾经提到，在有关英国驻北京大使亚美士德爵士使团的记载中，如果我记得没错的话，这位大使的一个随从就曾

59

因为乘坐这样的马车，在很短的旅行中死于颠簸。但既然这种交通方式速度最快，我决定这次就乘坐马车出行。几年来在中国乘坐马车旅行的经历已经让我胆大了不少，所以我并不害怕曾经击垮亚美士德使团的那种厄运。我舒舒服服地裹在中式棉衣里，缩成一团，挤进了马车，觉得自己就像是一件精美瓷器，裹在棉花里。收拾停当，我和北京的朋友们依依惜别。驾车人"啪"的一声挥起皮鞭，拉着悠扬的调子，赶着骡子，我们上路了。

I had made a contract with a cart firm to supply me with two carts to take me to Lanchou Fu, the capital of Kan-su, a distance of over thirteen hundred miles, in thirty-four days. For every day over the stipulated time I was to receive two ounces of silver (two taels), and for every day gained on the schedule time I was to pay them a bonus of the same amount. This arrangement worked perfectly. I experienced no delays on the route, and reached my destination two days ahead of time.

……

之前，我就和马车公司签了合同。他们为我提供两驾马车，负责把我带到甘肃省首府兰州府。行程距离一千三百多英里。合同规定，行程时间为三十五天。如果超出了规定时间，他们每天都会赔付我两盎司银子（相当于二两银子）。如果他们提前抵达目的地，我每天也要支付他们同样数量的银子，作为奖励。根据这种安排，事情进行得极为顺利！整个行程我一天都没有耽搁，甚至比预计时间还提前两天到达了目的地。

……

In the first stage of my journey, which took me across the western border of Northern China to the Koko-nor country, I was accompanied by one Chinese servant, a young rascal who prior to this had made a journey with Lieutenant Younghusband of the British army through Mongolia and

Turkestan and thence across the Mustagh pass to India. He was of scanty assistance to me, as I lived on what food I could purchase at the inns, and, speaking Chinese myself, I did not require his services as interpreter, in which capacity he may have rendered some aid to his former master, although the "pigeon English" jargon he spoke would have required more study to understand than the most difficult dialect in China.

在此次旅行的第一个阶段，我跨越华北的西部边界，来到了青海湖地区。在这段行程中，一个中国仆人和我做伴。在此之前，这个年轻的捣蛋鬼曾伴随英国陆军的弗朗西斯·荣赫鹏中尉，穿越蒙古和突厥斯坦，之后又穿越慕士塔格通道到达过印度。不过话说回来，一路上他也没帮我什么忙。因为我吃的东西都能在酒馆里买到，我本人又能说汉语，所以不需要他做翻译。他的翻译本事对之前的雇主来说可能还有些帮助。可对我来说，要想听懂他说的洋泾浜混杂方言，比学习中国最难懂的方言还费劲儿。

The route we followed between Peking and Hsi-an Fu is the great highway and artery of commerce between northeastern, central, and southwestern China, and travel over it presents no hardships: every few miles along the road one passes inns and eating-houses, and large towns are met with daily.

……

从北京到西安府我们选择的路线是连接中国东北、中部和西南地区的大路。这条公路同时也是一条繁忙的商业大动脉。这段行程我们可真是一点罪都没受。每走几英里，路边就能看到小酒馆和小吃铺。每天都能经过繁华的大镇子。

……

Baron von Richthofen was the first geologist to propound the theory, now universally adopted, that the loess of China owes its origin to the action of wind sweeping over the treeless steppes of Central Asia, removing the sand and dust eastward, the latter finally settling in the grass-covered districts of Northwestern China, the Koko-nor, and even Eastern Tibet. New vegetation was at once nourished, while its roots were raised by the constantly arriving deposit; the decay of old roots produced the lime-lined canals which impart to this material its peculiar characteristics [1].

冯·李希霍芬男爵是一位杰出的地质学家。他首次提出以下理论：中国黄土的形成是风力作用的结果。大风席卷了中亚荒芜广阔的大草原，将厚厚的黄土带到了中原。在大风移动的过程中，沙尘向东推移，最终在中国西北、青海湖和西藏东部植被覆盖的地区沉积下来。在那里，新的植被立刻得到了丰富的滋养，根部在不断吹来的沉积物滋润下日益茁壮。而老根部的腐烂则形成了带有石灰线纹的沟沟壑壑，别有一番味道 [2]。现在，上述理论已经得到了人们的广泛采用。

Through these loess beds I traveled with but few interruptions until I left China proper to enter the Koko-nor region, a distance of about 1200 miles. Generally speaking the traveling was most uninteresting, for the roads lay at the bottom of deep cuts and all view of the surrounding country was hidden from us.

......

我穿过黄土高原的谷底，一路行进顺利，期间基本没怎么耽搁。最终我离开了中原大地，进入了青海湖。此时，我的行程已经有一千二百英里左右。总的来说，这场旅行极端无趣，因为道路都在黄土沟壑的底部，所有迷人美丽的乡村景致都是看不到的。

......

We followed up the course of the Yellow River for a day and a half, and then, crossing the stream on a small ferryboat, entered the valley

---

[1]　See Richthofen's "China", Vol. I, p. 74.

[2]　参看李希特霍芬所著《中国》，第一卷，第 74 页。

of the Hsi-ning River, up which we journeyed for four days more, passing only one town on the way, the prefectural city of Nien-pei. In the mountains to the east of it gold washing is extensively carried on, although the profit derived therefrom seems to be very small. It is a common saying among the people that when a man tried in vain to make a livelihood by all conceivable methods he finally takes to washing gold.

我们沿着黄河流域走了一天半的时间，然后乘坐一艘小渡船，穿过溪流，进入西宁河（现称湟水河）河谷。沿着河谷，我们向上追溯了四天多。我们一路上只路过了一个镇子——府城碾伯。在县城东边的山区，普遍兴起了淘金热。不过，人们从中获得的利润似乎很少。当地人中有种很普遍的说法，如果一个人想尽办法都没法谋生，那他就只好去淘金了。

When some ten miles from Hsi-ning we crossed a wooden bridge to the right bank of the river, after which our road led through a narrow gorge in a range of granitic and schistose rocks which cuts the valley at right angles. The road here presented no more difficulty than is usually met with in such gorges, in fact not nearly so much as in those near Lao-ya-p'u. But listen to what Abbe Hue says of it in his charming *Souvenirs of a Journey in Tartary and Tibet.*

在距离西宁大约十英里的地方，我们跨过了一座木桥，走到河的右岸。之后，我们穿过一个狭窄的峡谷，在满是花岗岩和片状岩嶙峋林立的山脉中穿梭前行。整个河谷中，这样的石头犬牙交错，形成了一处处十分险峻的悬崖峭壁。不过，这里的路并不比我们平常见到的类似峡谷更难走。实际上，地势也比不上老鸦堡附近的那些峡谷凶险。可是，让我们来听听法国传教士古伯察（Evariste Régis Huc）神父在那部迷人的《鞑靼西藏旅行记》中是怎么描述的吧！

A day before reaching Si Ning we traveled over a most difficult and dangerous piece of road, where we often had to recommend ourselves to the protection of Divine Providence. We went amidst great boulders and beside a deep torrent where seething waters leaped at our feet. The abyss yawned beneath us and a slip would have sufficed to precipitate us into it. But chiefly did we tremble for our camels, so awkward and so heavy when walking in dangerous places. But in the end, thanks to God's bounty, we reached Si Ning without accident.

　　到达西宁的前一天，我们跋涉了一段最艰难颠簸、最危险的路段。一路上，我们不断向上帝祈祷，祈求他保佑我们平安。我们在巨大的岩石丛中穿行，来到一条水深流急的洪流旁，沸腾的水在我们的脚边跳跃。一眼望不见底的深渊似乎在我们脚下张开了血盆大口，似乎随时都能将我们吞噬。我们只要一不小心就会被抛入万劫不复的地狱。不过我们主要也是为这些骆驼们担心。在危险路段，这些原本就很笨重的牲畜就会变得更笨拙。不过，感谢上帝，我们最后有惊无险地到达了西宁，一点儿事故都没发生。

A clear case of distance lending enchantment to the view; for not only is the gorge a short one, but there is absolutely no danger in it, and the most awkward camel in the world could go through it on a run.

　　显然，这个例子很好地证明了距离产生美与魅力。说实话，这条峡谷并不长，也绝对没什么危险。世界上最笨拙的骆驼也能小跑着穿过峡谷。

We reached Hsi-ning Fu on the afternoon of February 6, and took up our quarters in a large inn in the suburbs; but we had hardly alighted when I was requested by the police to report to the authorities, show my passport, and tell them my plans, none of which did I in the least care to do. So at daylight next morning, having shaved my head and face and changed my Chinese gown for a big red cloth one like that worn by Mongols and Tibetans, and having made a few minor alterations in my dress, I left Hsi-ning with a party of K'alk'a Mongols with whom I had traveled for the last few days, and went to the famous lamasery of Kumbum, called by the Chinese T'ar-ssu, about twenty miles away, where there were no bothersome officials asking embarrassing questions and prying into one's affairs.

我们在 1889 年 2 月 6 号下午到达了西宁府，准备在郊区一个大客栈安顿下来。可是我们刚刚下马，当地捕快就立刻跑上来要求我向衙门汇报，呈交通关文牒，并告知我的计划。我对这些真的一点儿都不在乎。第二天黎明时分，我剃了头，又刮了刮脸，换下中式长褂，裹上了蒙古人和西藏人裹的那种大红布。在着装略作改变后，我和迦勒迦河（Kalka）的一群蒙古人离开了西宁。在过去的几天里，我们一直相伴旅行。我们一起前往距离西宁大概二十英里的著名喇嘛庙——塔尔寺。在这里，没什么烦人的官员问我们那些令人尴尬的问题，刺探我们的事儿。

The road thither was crowded with pilgrims, Mongols, Tibetans, and Sifans, all hurrying to witness the feast of the 15th of the first moon and the display of wonderful butter bas-reliefs, when the temple and the adjacent villages are filled with people from all the country round and from far-off Tibet, from Lh'asa, TrashiPunpo, and K'amdo, from Eastern Mongolia and from Turkestan.

在去往那里的路上，挤满了朝圣者，蒙古人、藏人和西番人（西番指中国西域地区）。他们都行色匆匆地赶往目的地，希望能够参加正月十五元宵节的盛事，亲眼看见酥油花（一种用酥油 / 黄油塑形像物的特殊技艺）这种虔诚的油塑艺术。每年的这个时候塔尔寺和临近的村落都会聚集着来自西藏各地的人们。有些人来自拉萨，有些来自扎什伦布寺，有些来自西藏东部的卡玛多，有些人甚至从更偏远的地区过来，还有些人来自蒙古东部和中亚。

THE BORDER-LAND OF CHINA: A JOURNEY THROUGH AN UNKNOWN LAND

中国边境：穿越无人之境的旅行

No longer were all the passers-by blue-gowned and long-queued Chinese, but people of different language and different dress. There were Mongols, some of them from Urga near Kiakhta or the remote Amoor provinces, dressed in greasy sheepskin gowns and big fur caps, or else in the yellow or red cloth ones of lamas. The women were hardly distinguishable from the men save those who, from coquetry, had put on their green satin gowns and head and neck ornaments of silver, so as to produce a sensation on entering Lusar, the suburb of Kumbum. With them were long strings of camels, many of them bearing gifts, sometimes of great value, for the temple. Then came parties of pilgrims tramping along in single file, each with a little load held by a light wooden frame fastened to his back. ... Many other queer people we saw as we rode along, T'u-ssu and K'amba, Panak'a and Salar, of all of whom I shall have to speak later.

我们目及之处不再只是身着蓝袍、留着长辫子的汉人，而是操着各种语言、穿着各种服饰、来自世界各地的人们。这当中的蒙古人有些来自边境小镇恰克图附近的库伦（乌兰巴托的旧称），有些来自遥远的阿穆尔省（现在的黑龙江省）。他们要么穿着油腻腻的羊皮大氅、戴着皮帽子，要么就裹着喇嘛穿的红黄僧袍。女人和男人看不出有什么分别。只有那些身着绿色绸缎长袍、头上和颈上戴着银饰的卖弄风骚的女人，才比较显眼。这些人在进入塔尔寺郊区（西藏安多地区）的鲁沙尔镇时，往往会引起轰动。陪同着这些女人的是一长队的骆驼。很多骆驼还驮着送给寺院的礼物，其中一些礼物尤为贵重。接着，排成一路纵队的朝圣者们迈着沉重的脚步前行着。每人背上都绑着一个很轻的木架子，里面装着少量的行李。……我们这一路行来，还遇到了很多古里古怪的行者，有土司人、巴塘人、康巴人、巴纳人、撒拉人。这些人，我过会儿就会谈到。

Our road led up a valley, towards a high black range of nude and jagged peaks, rising like a wall across its southern extremity, and which figures on our maps as the South Kokonor range. When about fifteen miles up we turned to the southwest, and crossing the low hills which here border it, we saw in the narrow valley of loess formation lying at our feet a straggling village built on the steep sides of a hill at the foot of which two small streams met. ... On the flat roofs of the village houses sat men and women gossiping, spinning yarn, or spreading out manure to dry. This was Lusar, the suburb, as it were, of Kumbum. As I stood on top of the hill leading down to the village I looked to my left and there were the golden roofs and spires of the temples with walls of green or red, and over the hillside roundabout were long, irregular lines of low, flat-roofed houses, partly hidden behind clean whitewashed walls, the homes of three thousand odd lamas who live in this great sanctuary of the Tibetan and Mongol faith. On the hill slope between the village and the lamasery was the fair-ground, where a motley crowd was moving to and fro, where droves of yaks and strings of camels were continually arriving, while scattered about farther away were the traveling tents of those who preferred their ordinary dwellings to the small, dingy rooms to be rented in the lamasery or at Lusar.

我们一路走到一个河谷，对面是一片高耸乌黑、呈锯齿状分布的光秃秃峰峦，在最南端像面墙一样高耸而起。在我们的地图上，这片地区正是南青海湖山脉。在上行了大约十五英里之后，我们朝西南方行进，跨过了和此处接壤的低圆小山丘。在狭窄河谷的黄土层中，我们看到脚下坐落着一个无规则散乱排列的村子。这个村落建在一个陡峭的山坡上，山脚下两条涓涓细流汇聚于一处。……在村舍平坦的屋顶上，坐着农夫农妇，在那里七嘴八舌地八卦着什么。他们或是纺着线，或是把拾到的粪摆出来晒。这里就是鲁沙尔（Lusar），可以说是塔尔寺的郊区。我站在小山顶上，俯瞰村子，忽然在左方看到了寺庙的金色屋顶和尖塔，还有红墙绿瓦。在山坡周围，坐落着一长排错落参差的低矮平顶房子。在刷着白灰的干净院墙后面，这些房舍若隐若现。在这里，居住着三千多位喇嘛。这里对西藏和蒙古来说是伟大的佛教圣地。在村落和喇嘛庙之间的山坡上，是一个集市。各色人群出出进进，热闹非凡。不断有成群牦牛和一队队的骆驼来到这里。在稍远处散落着旅行者们的帐篷。他们宁可住在这种普通住宅，也不愿租住喇嘛庙或鲁沙尔脏兮兮的小房子。

It was the day after my arrival at Lusar, the twelfth of the first moon, when the Chinese in every town and village all over the Empire celebrate the Dragon festival (lung-tung hui) that I made my first acquaintance with the place. The streets of the village were crowded with people dressed in their holiday best, and all pressing on towards the Chinese temple at the foot of the hill where the feast was to begin. The theatrical representation was without interest, but the spectators were delightful. On one side were squatting a group of Rongwa Tibetan men and women in high-collared sheepskin or cloth gowns trimmed with leopard skins. On their heads were little pointed red caps with lambskin borders, or dark red turbans draped in loose but graceful folds. The women dressed like the men except that their hair fell from under their little caps over their shoulders and backs in numberless small plaits like cloaks, the plaits held together by broad bands of ribbon on which were sewed cowries, pieces of money, coral, turquoise or glass beads. The day was warm and the men and women had slipped their right arms out of their gowns, showing their bronzed and muscular forms undefiled by any acquaintance with water, to say nothing of soap.

我抵达鲁沙尔后的第二天是正月十二。举国上下，从乡村到城镇，中国人都在庆祝即将到来的元宵节（龙灯会）。就是在这样的日子里，我首次造访了塔尔寺。镇子的街道上挤满了穿着节日盛装的人们，都朝着山脚下的汉族寺庙进发。在那里会有一场盛事。其实，戏剧的再现形式没什么意思，但是观众们都很高兴。道路的一侧蹲坐着一群绒瓦藏族男女。他们穿着高领的羊皮外套，或是豹纹边儿的布制大褂。他们头上或是戴着红色的尖顶小帽，帽子边缘是羊羔皮做的，或是绑着宽松的深红色头巾，颇为优雅。女人着装和男人没什么不同，只是她们的头发从小帽子后面飘散下来，搭在肩膀和后背上。她们的头发编成无数条小辫子，就像一个个小斗篷。她们用宽大的丝带绑着辫子，丝带上缝有五颜六色的贝壳、小钱币、珊瑚、绿松石或玻璃珠子。天气很暖和，这些善男信女都把右臂从长袍中伸了出来，露出了古铜色的肌肉和健壮的身形。他们常年没有经历过水的荡涤，就更不要说用香皂清洁了。

Near them stood some T'u-ssu in dress closely resembling the Chinese, only they wore their gowns short and full in Tibetan fashion; the women with bright red handkerchiefs around their heads, and long violet gowns of Chinese pattern.

在这些人附近，站着一些土司人，从着装上看和汉族人很像。只是他们把袍子穿得较短，穿法也完全是西藏风格。女人头上围着鲜红色的手帕，穿着紫色长袍，上面印着汉族图案。

Mongols of the Koko-nor and the Ts'aidam were not wanting. They have adopted to a great extent the dress of their Tibetan neighbors: like the ass in the lion's skin, they doubtless think themselves more formidable when thus arrayed. Their women, when not married, dress their hair in Tibetan fashion, but the married ones wear two heavy tresses, falling on each side of the face and incased in black embroidered satin. K'alk'a

Mongols from Eastern Mongolia were there also, the richness of their dress and the softer tones of their speech distinguishing them from their poorer and harsher-spoken kinsmen of the West.

在这里，来自青海湖和柴达木盆地的蒙古人也不少。他们在很大程度上已经采纳了藏族邻居们的服饰风格。就像是狐假虎威的狐狸，他们毫无疑问认为，自己穿着这种衣服看起来会所向披靡。女人们如果还没结婚，就会像西藏人一样绑起头发。那些结了婚的则会把头发分成两个厚实浓密的发绺，分别放在脸颊两侧，再用黑色绣花丝缎绑起来。这里还有来自蒙古东部的迦勒迦蒙古人。他们服饰炫目多彩，说话语气柔和。这些特点把他们和西部较为贫穷、语气较粗哑的同族人区分开来。

Beside me stood some tall, swarthy-looking men with thin features and aquiline noses, dressed in dark violet gowns, and, unlike the Koko-nor Tibetan, with long queues and turquoise ear-rings in the left ear. They were traders from Lh'asa and Trashil'unpo, and had come from Tankar, where they had left their camels and goods, to see the festival.

在我旁边，还站着一些高挑瘦削、皮肤黝黑的鹰钩鼻男人。他们穿着深紫色长袍。和青海湖的藏族人不同，他们梳着长辫子，左耳朵上还佩戴着绿松石耳坠儿。他们是来自拉萨和扎什伦布寺的商人。他们把骆驼和货物寄放在东科寺（Tankar，现称为湟源），来此地观看节日盛事。

But it would require a whole chapter to describe the various tribes represented at Lusar that day. One whose wild, fierce looks, and whose long swords, on which their hand always rested, fixed my attention from the first. They were K'ambas, or Hung-mao-tzu, "Red capped men", as the Chinese of Kan-su call this people, natives of Eastern Tibet. Their dress is a dirty sheepskin gown hanging in large folds below their waists and hardly reaching to their knees; their boots, with rawhide soles and tops of bright-colored cloth, are held by garters below the knee. They wear no headdress. Their long, tangled hair, falling over their shoulders and cut in a fringe to their eyes, is so matted and thick that they do not feel the want of a better head-cover.

……

但要想描述那天在鲁沙尔出现的各个部落，可能需要另辟一个新的章节。一个看起来野蛮凶狠、手上握着长剑的部落从一开始就吸引了我注意力。他们是康巴人，或称为红帽族。住在甘肃的汉族人就是这样称呼西藏东部的土著部落。他们的服装是脏兮兮的羊皮大袍子，腰部以下垂着巨大的褶皱，几乎盖不到膝盖处。他们穿的靴子鞋底是生牛皮的，靴面由鲜艳夺目的布制成。他们用吊袜带绑住靴子，系在膝盖下方。他们不戴头饰，长头发乱蓬蓬的，垂在肩膀上。他们留着刘海，露出双眼，浓厚茂密的头发乱成一团。也许他们觉得，除了头发，再找不到更好、更合适的头饰啦。

……

Though the street scenes at Lusar were full of varied interest, I was impatient to see Kumbum and its temples; so we crossed over to the other side of the valley, and, pushing our way through the crowd of peddlers and people of every description who thronged the hillside, passed under a high white monument offering holder or receptacle and entered the lamasery grounds. A broad road, now crowded with people buying and selling every variety of goods, led to a building with red walls and green-tiled roof, the convent treasure-house. Near it was another smaller building with a garden in front inclosed within high walls. It was the temple of the famous tree which grows on the spot where the hair of Tsongk'apa had fallen when he was shaved and consecrated to the church by his mother. On each of its leaves is an outline figure of the god. The lamas say that this tree is a white sandal-wood, but it is probably a lilac. This appeared to me the more likely, as I was told that it bears large bunches of violet flowers in the spring. The leaves which fall from the tree are carefully gathered up and sold to visitors, who keep them as charms or use them as medicine. Those I got were so broken that I could distinguish nothing on them; but I was assured by unbelieving Mohammedans that the picture is clearly discernible on the leaves, and that they are "valuable curios", as they put it.

虽然鲁沙尔的街头景致充满趣味，但我无心留恋，迫不及待想要亲眼看看塔尔寺和其中各处庙宇。我们跨到河谷的另一侧，穿梭于山坡上聚集的小商贩和各色人群中间，从一座高耸的白色纪念碑下经过，最终进入了喇嘛庙圣境。这座纪念碑的用处或是支撑物，或是用来摆放花朵。原本是一条宽宽的道路上，现在却挤满了出售和购买各种商品的人，熙熙攘攘、人声鼎沸。这条道路通向一座建筑，红墙绿瓦的屋顶着实引人注目。那是寺院的藏宝阁。旁边是一座小点儿的建筑物，围在高高的围墙里，建筑物的前方有个迷人的小花园。在这座庙宇中，长着一棵闻名天下的树。据说，宗喀巴（藏传佛教格鲁派的创始人）的妈妈将他奉献给寺院，又为他剃度。这棵树的生长地点正是他剃度时毛发掉落之处。每一片树叶上都有佛的轮廓图。喇嘛们说，这棵树是白檀香木。不过，我觉得这很有可能就是紫丁香。在我看来，这似乎更可能接近事实，因为我听说在春天这种树会长出大簇大簇的紫色花朵。寺庙里的僧人小心翼翼地将树上落下的叶子捡拾起来，卖给游客们。他们将这种叶子作为护身符或是药材。我得到的那些叶子已经很破旧了，所以上面的图画看不清楚。不过，就连不信佛的伊斯兰教徒也向我保证，叶子上的图像清晰可辨。用他们自己的话来说，这些都是"很有价值的古董"。

On this my first visit to the lamasery I could not visit the treasure-house, which was only opened on the 15th, when the Chinese ambassador, or Hsi-ning Amban, as he is commonly called, visited the place; but we were shown the chief temple, whose golden roofs had attracted my attention when I was approaching Lusar. It is in its main features built in Chinese style, and does not differ essentially from the Buddhist temples seen at Peking and in other localities in Northern China. In front is a spacious courtyard, and the temple is raised some eight feet above its level. Those who wish to worship before the holy shrines stand on a broad plank walk in the courtyard at the base of the temple and there they make their prostrations. The deep grooves worn in the planks by the feet and hands of the devotees testify to the popularity of this gymnastic form of worship. In the dimly lighted temple we could distinguish only the three principal shrines, the central one that of Gautama Buddha, that on his right Tsongk'apa, and that on his left Dipankara Buddha.

在初次造访喇嘛庙时，我没能进藏宝阁参观。因为藏宝阁只在阴历十五才开放，每当那天清政府的派驻人员西宁驻藏大臣会来此地参观。不过，我们还是有幸参观了正殿——大金瓦殿。还没到鲁沙尔的时候，吸引我目光的那片金碧辉煌的屋顶正是来自此处。主要特点方面，正殿的建筑风格是汉族风格，和我在北京和中国北方其它地方见到的那些佛教寺庙没什么本质的区别。寺庙前部是一个宽敞的庭院，寺庙高约八英尺。那些希望在圣殿中虔诚祈祷的善男信女站在宽厚的木板上，走进庭院。在神圣寺庙的脚下，他们五体投地、叩头跪拜。这些信徒们长年累月跪拜。他们的手脚在木板上已经留下了深深的凹槽。这一切都证明，这种祭拜方式是多么普遍。在光线昏暗的庙宇里，我们只能区分出三个主要神龛。中间那个塑像是佛教创始人乔达摩（佛陀，或释迦摩尼）。他的右边是宗喀巴，左边是燃灯佛。

To the right of this gold-roofed temple is the temple of Tsongk'apa called the Je k'ang. It has two superposed roofs, covered with green tiles and supported by red-lacquered pillars. The lower wall of the building is covered with green tiles and a narrow walk leads around it. In front of the temple, within a little wooden paling, is another "white sandal-wood tree", on the branches of which hang numbers of ceremonial scarfs offered by the faithful. My Chinese servant, who accompanied me in my walk, nearly got into trouble here. We had entered the temple inclosure on its left side, and started to walk around, keeping it on our right hand. He, not knowing or forgetting that to walk around a sacred building keeping it on one's left side is sacrilegious, began his walk in the wrong direction. He had not gone two steps when he was pulled up by a lot of lamas and visitors and started off in the right way, with some forcible remarks about his improper conduct in holy places.

这座金色屋顶的大金瓦殿右侧是宗喀巴祠庙，被称为大银塔。大银塔上有两个叠加屋顶，上面铺着绿瓦，下部有红漆柱子作为支撑。这座建筑物的低墙铺满了绿瓦，周围环绕着一条很窄的小径。在寺庙前方，有另外一棵白檀香树，树旁围着一圈小小的木栅栏。在树杈上，信徒们挂上了数不清的丝带、丝巾，用来祈祷和祈福。我的中国仆人陪着我转来转去，可他差点儿惹上大麻烦。事情的经过是这样的：我们已经从左侧走进寺庙围地，正准备四处转转，保持寺庙在自己的右手边。这时，不知这仆人是不知道，还是忘记了这一点：如果从右侧绕着神圣建筑走动，那可是亵渎神明的大不敬之举。总之，他走错了方向。不过走了还没两步，喇嘛和游人们就把他拦了下来，要求他从正确的方向走。这些人在旁边指指点点、评头论足，对他在圣地的不当行为颇有微词。

Tsongk'apa, to whom Kumbum owes its origin, deserves more than a passing mention, for he is the founder of the form of Buddhist worship which prevails throughout Mongolia and the greater part of Tibet in short, of modern lamaism. He was born A. D. 1360, near the place where

Kumbum now stands, his parents belonging to the Amdo Tibetans, who still inhabit the country. At the age of sixteen he began his theological studies, but the following year, by the advice of his teacher, he went to Lh'asa, where he soon became a master in all the branches of Buddhist learning. Abbé Hue, struck by the many points of resemblance between the lamaist and Catholic churches, was convinced, when he heard that the first teacher of Tsongk'apa had a long nose, that he was one of the Catholic missionaries who at that time had penetrated Central Asia in large numbers. The length of a nose is but a poor foundation for such an important theory, and, even if we accept noses as criterions, we would find that those of the people of Turkestan are quite as long, if not longer, than our own. We have, however, the authority of Marco Polo for it that in his time (latter part of the thirteenth century) there were some Christians at Hsi-ning (Sinju), and we know that in the fourteenth century Christianity flourished at Peking. But this is no proof that Tsongk'apa, who when only seventeen went to Lh'asa, where Christianity certainly was not to be found, had ever seen a Catholic church or heard the Gregorian chant, and the whole subject requires much more study before we can draw any conclusion, and above all it requires unprejudiced students who have no preconceived theories to demonstrate.

塔尔寺是为了纪念中国藏传佛教格鲁派（黄教）创始人宗喀巴而建。这个人物可是值得一提。他所创建的佛教敬拜形式，即现代喇嘛教，在整个蒙古和西藏大部分地区都大为盛行。他生于公元 1360 年，出生地就在今天的塔尔寺附近。他的父母都是安多藏民。现在，安多藏民仍旧在那一地区生息繁衍着。十六岁那年，他开始了佛学研究。第二年，听从老师的建议，他去了拉萨。在那儿，他很快就成了佛学所有分支教派的大师。法国传教士古伯察神父对于喇嘛庙和天主教堂之间的很多相似之处都曾十分惊讶。不过，后来他听说宗喀巴的第一位老师是个长鼻子的天主教传教士，便茅塞顿开了。

当时，大批天主教传教士曾深入中亚，传播信仰。这位传教士便是其中之一。不过，对于这么重要的理论来说，鼻子长度这个证据却不那么靠谱。即使将鼻子长度作为标准，也会发现中亚人的鼻子和我们的也差不多长，甚至比我们的还要长。不过，我们还有马可·波罗游记这个权威。在他生活的年代（十三世纪下半叶），西宁确实有些基督徒。我们知道，十四世纪基督教在北京繁荣发展。不过，并没有证据表明，在十七岁时就来到拉萨的宗喀巴曾见过天主教堂，或是聆听过格利高利圣咏。因为当时在拉萨是绝对找不到基督教踪迹的。要想得出结论，我们得进一步仔细研究这个话题。在这方面，只有客观公平、不带任何偏见、不依赖于任何先入之见的学者才能胜任。

Hue gives a long list of points of resemblance in the dress, habits, and ceremonies of the lamas and Catholic priests, comprising the use of the crozier, miter, dalmatic, censer held by five chains, holy water, chanting, exorcisms, worship of saints, celibacy, retreats, fasts, and litanies; but he omits one which I think very curious. When a person is dying a lama will frequently be called in, to administer to him the dro män, or "going medicine". With some of his spittle he anoints the forehead, the palms of the hands, and the soles of the feet of the dying person, to the end that he may have a rapid transmigration. Where did this idea of extreme unction come from? And where did they get that of drinking holy water as a cure for bodily pains, a habit frequently met with among uneducated Catholics?

古伯察神父从服饰、习惯和仪式等方面，列出了长长一串喇嘛和天主教牧师之间的相似点，其中包括牧杖的使用、主教法冠、法衣、五链香炉、圣水、诵经、驱魔、敬拜圣人、独身主义、隐居所、斋戒和连祷。不过，他还是漏掉了我觉得很有趣的一点。当一个人快死时，人们经常会叫喇嘛来，给他喂送"去药"。喇嘛把自己的唾液涂抹在将死之人的前额、手掌和脚底上，好让他早点轮回。这种给临终者涂油礼的仪式从何而来呢？他们又是从哪里学到了喝圣水治愈肉体疼痛的做法呢？没受过教育的天主教徒们也常有这种习惯。

If we can say nothing definite on this interesting subject, we have ample information concerning the origin and history of the lamaist church founded by Tsongk'apa. He, as we have seen, went to Lh'asa at an early age; there he studied, preached, reformed, and finally transmigrated into the person of Gédun drupa, who founded the Trashil'unpo lamasery in 1446 and became the first of the series of incarnated gods known as Panch'en rinpoché, although native works say that the first pontiff bearing this title was born in 1567. Becoming afterwards incarnate in Gédun jyats'o, he returned to Lh'asa and was made head of the great Drébung lamasery of that place. His successor was So-nam jyats'o, "the Sea of Charity", and all the succeeding incarnations have had the word jya-ts'o (i.e. sea) as a portion of their style. This pontiff visited the Mongol conqueror Altan Khan, and he, imagining that jya-ts'o (in Mongol talé) was his name, addressed him as Talé lama, and the name has been used ever since by Chinese and Mongols to designate the head of the lamaist hierarchy; but the Tibetans speak of him as "The victorious ocean", or "The most excellent protector". He is held to be an incarnation of the Merciful God who watches over the world, Shenrezig with the thousand heads and thousand eyes. In China this god has become a goddess and is called Kuan-yin, and half of the representations one sees of her show her holding an infant in her arms, and looking for all the world like the conventional statue of the Virgin Mary. I once came across a Chinese book entitled "The Fifty Manifestations of Kuan-yin". One picture showed her likeness as she appeared to an old man in Shan-hsi, another the form under which she had shown herself to a devout priest, and in one she had appeared to a poor laborer as Peter the Great of Russia, for there was the picture of the great emperor in breastplate and wig and with a marshal's baton in his hand. In what strange semblance will Kuan-yin make her next appearance? Will it be as Washington or as Gladstone, both of whose pictures I have seen in out-of-the-way places in China?

如果关于这个有趣的话题，我们还没什么定论，那至少我们有足够的信息能了解宗喀巴所建造的这座喇嘛庙的来历与变迁。前边我们已经说过，他在很年轻的时候就去了拉萨，并在那里学习、讲道、进行改良活动，并最终成为转世活佛——根敦朱巴（一世达赖喇嘛）。此人在 1446 年创建了扎什伦布寺，并担任该寺第一任班禅活佛。不过，当地的书籍记载第一位享有此头衔的教宗出生于 1567 年。之后，继任他的转世活佛为二世达赖根敦嘉措。此人回到了拉萨，并被任命为哲蚌寺的大住持。他的继任是三世达赖喇嘛索南嘉措，意为"慈善之海"。所有继任转世活佛的名字中都有"嘉措"一词，意为"海洋"。这位主教曾拜访蒙古征服者俺答汗。他认为嘉措（蒙古语中即"达赖"，意为"海洋"）是自己的名字，并称自己为"达赖喇嘛"。自此之后，汉族人和蒙古人就都开始使用"达赖喇嘛"一词，指代喇嘛教等级制度中的宗教领袖。不过，西藏人将他称为"胜利的海洋"，或是"完美的庇护者"。他被认为是仁慈天神转世，千头千眼地注视着整个世界——仙乃日。在中原，这个神被描绘成一位女性，名曰观世音菩萨。在她的形象中，有一半都描绘着她怀抱一个婴儿，俯瞰人世间。这个形象颇像圣母玛利亚的传统塑像。我曾看过一本名为《观音五十造像》的中文书。一张画像是她在山西向一个老人显身，另一张画像是她向一个虔诚的和尚显形，第三张则是她以俄国彼得大帝的样貌向一个穷人现身。因为，这张画像描绘了这位大帝穿着护胸甲，戴着假发，手中还拿着元帅杖。在下次显露"真"颜时，谁知道观世音又会采取什么奇怪的外形呢？她会不会以华盛顿或格莱斯顿的外形出现呢？说实话，我在中国偏远地区都曾见过这两位政治家的画像。

We were walking homeward from the temple when suddenly the crowd scattered to the right and left, the lamas running for places of hiding with cries of "Gékor lama, gékor lama!" and we saw striding towards us six or eight lamas with a black stripe painted across their foreheads and another around their right arms, "black lamas", the people call them, and armed with heavy whips, with which they belabored any one who came within their reach. Behind them walked a stately lama in robes of finest cloth and with head clean shaved. He was a "gékor", a lama censor or provost, whose duty it was to see that the rules of the lamasery were strictly obeyed, and who, in conjunction with two colleagues, like him appointed by the abbot for a term of three years, tries all lamas for whatever crimes or breach of the rules they may have committed. This one had heard that there were peep-shows, Punch and Judy shows, roulette tables, and other prohibited amusements on the fair-grounds, and he was on his way with his lictors to put an end to the scandal. I followed in his wake and saw the peep-show whose special attraction, I am sorry to say, were European (Belgian) obscene pictures knocked down, Punch and Judy laid out mangled beside it, the owners whipped and put to flight, and the majesty of ecclesiastical law and morality duly vindicated.

我们正要从寺庙回落脚之处，突然间人群向左右两边散开。喇嘛们一边大喊着"审查喇嘛！审查喇嘛来了！"一边四散寻找藏身之处。紧跟着，我们就看到六个或八个喇嘛迈着步子朝我们走来。他们的额头上画着一条黑道，右臂上也画着一条黑道。人们称他们为"黑喇嘛"。他们手中拿着沉重的鞭子。谁要是不知好歹冲撞了他们，肯定会被痛揍一顿。在他们身后，走来了一位气宇轩昂的喇嘛。他身上穿的袍子布料极为精美，他的头也剃得精光。他就是个"审查

喇嘛"，即喇嘛检查员或监督官。他的职责是查看寺庙的各项规章
制度是否得到了严格的遵守。他和两位同事都由住持任命，任期三
年。三人一同对喇嘛们有可能犯下的罪行或打破戒律的行为进行审
判。这个喇嘛听说此圣地居然出现了西洋镜、木偶戏表演、轮盘赌桌，
以及其他严令禁止的娱乐活动，所以就带着扈从前来调查这些丑闻。
我好奇地跟在他身后。我不得不说，西洋镜里主要吸引人们眼球的
是欧洲（比利时的）色情图片。它的下场很惨，被摔了个粉碎。木
偶戏的道具被砍得乱七八糟、七零八落。这些物件儿的主人遭受了
很重的鞭刑，不得不仓皇逃窜。看来，僧院律法和道德准则的神圣
得到了维护和巩固。

On the morning of the fifteenth of the first moon (February 14) I
went, in company with a lama friend, to see the treasure-house and the
other sights which I had been prevented from seeing on my first visit.
On the panels of the gates opening into the yard of the building were
painted human skins, the hands, feet, and head hanging to them and all
reeking with blood, these to frighten all evil-doers, most likely, and make
their flesh creep at the very thought of what might befall them if they
tried to rob the place. Then on the walls of the yard, and protected by a
broad roof, were painted numbers of the guardian angels in their hideous
trappings of snakes, human skins, skulls, and bones, wallowing in blood
and surrounded by flames, and escorted by imps more ghastly than them
with heads of bulls, hogs, dogs, or eagles. The building was small and
very dark, so only with great difficulty could we distinguish the curious
things with which it was filled. Bowls of silver, ewers of gold, images
of the gods in gold, silver, and bronze, pictures, beautifully illuminated
manuscripts, carpets, satin hangings, cloisonné vases, and incense
burners enough to fill a museum. One big silver bowl was pointed out
to me with a bullet hole through it, made during the late Mohammedan

rebellion, when the lamasery was attacked, and the lamas with gun and sword defended their temples and treasures, and were killed by hundreds on the steps of the sanctuary or beside their burning houses. The Mohammedans spared the temples and the sacred sandal-wood trees, not even taking the gold tiles from the chief temple; a most extraordinary piece of sentimentalism on their part, or rather a miraculous intervention of the gods to preserve their holy place.

正月十五那天（公历 1889 年 2 月 14 日）的早晨，我在一位喇嘛朋友的陪同下，去参观了藏宝阁和其他一些初次拜访时候没能有幸得见的处所。在通向藏宝阁庭院大门的镶板上绘有人皮、人手、人脚。吊起来的人头令人惊悚地低垂着。所有这些都沾满了鲜血。这种可怖场景的目的是吓退所有作恶者。如果有人试图抢夺财物，看到这种场景，他们肯定会吓得毛骨悚然、不敢妄动。院墙上面绘有佛教护法天神的形象，另外还铺上了保护性的宽屋顶。这些天神身上缠绕着蛇、披着人皮、挂着骷髅和尸骸，长发披面，鲜血淋漓。他们身处团团烈焰，旁边还有小鬼们护卫。这些小鬼面目狰狞、更加阴森苍白，长着公牛、猪、狗或鹰的头。这个建筑物面积很小、颇为阴暗，所以我们费了很大劲儿才区分出里面特有的物件儿。银碗、金制大口水壶，金制、银制和铜制的各种佛像，画像、点缀精美的手稿、挂毯、绸缎挂饰、景泰蓝花瓶、香炉等等，应有尽有。这些物品几乎能与一个博物馆的藏品相媲美。有人给我指出了一个大银碗，碗上还留有一个弹孔。这个弹孔无声地诉说着上次伊斯兰教徒的反叛。在这次反叛中，塔尔寺受到袭击。喇嘛们都拿着刀枪，捍卫着自己的寺庙和财物。很多喇嘛或是在叛徒跨入圣殿时被杀死，或是与他们被烧毁的房屋同归于尽。不过，伊斯兰教徒并没有烧毁寺庙，也留下了那些象征神圣的檀香树。他们甚至都没有碰主殿的金砖银瓦。在这次行动中，似乎他们也表现出了一丝感伤悲悯的情怀。也有可能，是那些佛和神奇迹般地插手，保留了这一圣殿。

A little later on the Hsi-ning Amban and the high Chinese authorities of this part of the province arrived to see the butter bas-reliefs to be exposed that evening. The lamas, squatting on the ground, lined the road for more than half a mile, and through the midst of them the Amban and his suite passed, his well-mounted escort carrying bright-colored pennants on the ends of their lances, with trumpet blasts echoed back by the deep-sounding convent conch-shells.

稍晚一些时候，西宁驻藏大臣和这一地区的汉族高级长官来到这里，参观傍晚即将展示的油塑。喇嘛们蹲坐在地上，沿路排成一排，长度有一英里多。驻藏大臣及其随从气宇轩昂地从喇嘛中间走过。他的随从们个个端坐在马上，手举长矛。长矛的两端还系着色彩鲜艳的三角旗。这一队人马吹起威武的号角。寺庙里雄浑的法螺声似乎也作出回应。

二、1908 年达赖喇嘛北京之行的有关文献资料

有关 1908 年十三世达赖喇嘛访问北京觐见光绪皇帝和慈禧太后以及柔克义与达赖喇嘛及其特使会晤的情况，柔克义保存了相当丰富的档案资料，这些资料主要包括：

（一）柔克义写给西奥多·罗斯福的两封信件

信一

AMERICAN LEGATION,
PEKING, CHINA.
June 30, 1908
中国，北京，美国驻中国北京
公使馆，1908 年 6 月 30 日

Dear Mr. President:
尊敬的总统先生：

I have just had such an unique and interesting experience that I cannot forbear writing to you at once about it.
我忍不住立刻与您分享我最近一次独特而有趣的经历。

83

You remember that some days before the British expedition to Tibet in 1904 entered Lhasa, the Tale Lama fled from his capital and withdrew to the north, going finally to a place on the northern border of Mongolia called Urga. Here, —or rather in this vicinity— he resided until about a year ago, when he again came south across Mongolia and stopped at the great lamasery of Kumbum, near the Koko nor. Some months ago he left this place with some three hundred attendants and came to another great Buddhist centre called Wu-t'ai shan, in the province of Shansi, west of here. Here he is now staying. Shorting after my arrival in Peking in 1905, the Tale Lama sent two agents to Peking, both lamas of high rank, to report to him on conditions from time to time and enable him to shape his movement accordingly. He gave them a letter to me and sent me some presents. He said he had heard of my travels in Tibet and that I had learned the language of his country and read its literature. He bespoke my friendship for his agents and asked me to give them my opinion on what I thought he had better do, — return to Tibet at once or wait until the

-3-

was at a comparatively short distance from Peking, if I could go see him and thank him for his kindness to me and for the good opinion he entertained of me. He said that the Tale Lama would be much pleased to receive me and urged me to make the journey.

On the 15th of this month, there being no pressing work in the Legation, I set out with a couple of mule litters and a mule pack train and in five days, across the Chihli plain and the mountains to the west of it, I came to Wu-t'ai shan, where I had been once before, some twenty-three years ago.

The day after my arrival my friend, the lama agent of the Tale Lama, met me there and at once arranged for my reception by His Holiness for the next day (19th of June). The temple in which the Tale Lama is staying is on the top of a rather high and precipitous hill and a long flight of marble steps leads up to it. At the top of the steps is the gate to the temple; here I found the Tale Lama's body guard, armed with rough Martini rifles made in Lhasa, drawn up on

-4-

one side of the path leading from the gate to a small pavilion covered with blue tiles, and on the other the Chinese guard sent to protect him by the Government during his stay at the Wu-t'ai shan. A large number of Tibetan officials, lamas and laymen, were waiting at the gate for me and a couple of them arranged in my hands the ceremonial scarf (khtag, in Tibetan), which it is customary for guests to present to their hosts, a very large one of which I had brought with me.

I was then led by two lamas to the pavilion in which the Tale Lama was to receive me, a small building with two rooms and a corridor between them. A yellow silk curtain hung before the door of the room to the right; this was raised and I saw the Tale Lama seated in an arm chair on a slightly raised platform. His appearance took me absolutely by surprise. I had imagined a rather ascetic looking youth, bent by constantly sitting bow-legged on cushions, with a yellow complexion and a far-away meditative look. On the contrary I found a man of thirty-three, with a very bright face, rather dark brown, a moustache and a small tuft of hair under his lower lip. His eyes

eyes were large, rather prominent and obliquely set; his eyebrows rising slightly towards the temples gave him a rather *maussade* expression. His mouth was large, his teeth were white and perfect. His head was bare and as it had not been shaved for some days it added to the general outlandishness of his appearance. He was dressed in an imperial yellow satin gown and the which shawl all lamas wear and which hangs over the left shoulder and passes around the body, was of bright vermillion silk. His boots were yellow with blue braiding. His ears were large, but well-shaped; his hands good and thin.

I stood before him, bowed, and placed the scarf I had in my hands at his feet and he put the one he held on my out-stretched hands. Then I took off my hat and was asked to sit in an armchair placed in front of him. The only persons present were two attendants, an abbot who acted as interpreter, and Mr. Maskins of our Legation, who accompanied me.

An attendant brought in a cup of tea for the Tale Lama, who touches it to his lips; then a

cup was brought for me and placed on a little table beside me. After a while a bowl of sweetened rice was brought him and then one to me. Then a low table was placed before me with cakes, dried fruits, sweets, etc., on it.

The Tale Lama first asked me a number of questions concerning my journey from Peking, my age, how long I had been in China, etc. He spoke very low to the abbot who stood before him and he in turn repeated in Chinese what His Holiness had said.

After that he said that he had heard much about me and was most pleased to see me. He especially alluded to the fact that he had heard at once that I spoke his language. I replied to him in Tibetan this time and much to his satisfaction, as his eyes brightened and he gave a smile which showed all his teeth. After about a half hour's conversation he said that this was my first and formal visit to him, but that he hoped that I could remain at the Wu-t'ai shan a few days longer, so that he could see

British had completely evacuated the country.

您还记得吧？1904 年英国的西藏远征军进入拉萨的几天前，达赖喇嘛从都城逃走向北边退去。他最后跑到了蒙古北边界一个叫库伦（蒙古国首都乌兰巴托的旧称）的地方。他就在那里，或是在那附近的某个地方，一直居住到大概一年以前。之后，他又穿过蒙古，向南挺进，直到青海湖附近的塔尔寺这座喇嘛庙才停了下来。几个月前，他带着大约三百名随从离开这里，去往另一个佛教圣地五台山。这个地方在北京这儿的西边。他现在就住在那里。1905 年我刚到北京不久，达赖喇嘛就派了两个信使来。这两个代表都是地位很高的喇嘛，要随时向他汇报事情进展情况，好让他能据此安排自己的行动。他让二位喇嘛给我捎来一封信和一些礼物。他说，他听闻了我的西藏之旅，也听说我学过藏语，阅读过藏文文献。他希望我能友善地对待他的两位代表，还请我向二人谈谈我认为他应该怎么办才好——是立刻返回西藏，还是等待英国人完全撤离后再返回。

The agents of the Tale Lama proved most interesting men and I saw them frequently in 1905 and subsequent years.

打过交道以后，我发现达赖喇嘛的两位代表真的很有趣。1905 年我曾多次见过二人，之后的几年中也曾多次和他们打交道。

When I got back here from leave in May of this year, one of them (the other had died shortly before) came to see me and brought me another letter from the Tale Lama and some presents. I told him that I would be much gratified, now that His Holiness was at a comparatively short distance from Peking, if I could go see him and thank him for his kindness to me and for the good opinion he entertained of me. He said that the Tale Lama would be much pleased to receive me and urged me to make the journey.

今年 5 月份，我假期结束回到这里。其中一个代表（另一个很不幸刚刚去世）来看我，并给我带来了喇嘛的另一封信和一些礼物。我告诉这位代表，我十分感激喇嘛的好意。我也询问特使，既然尊贵的喇嘛离北京不太远，那我是不是应该去拜见一下，

-9-

oblige him. This he said he thoroughly understood and said that I could talk to his agents at Peking as to himself and that it would be correctly reported to him.

He then asked me as if I had the photograph of "My Emperor". I said I had at Peking and he requested that I send it to him. This I am doing to-day.

The Tale Lama then gave me a gilt image of the Buddha and a large ceremonial scarf to present to you from him, after which he gave me a number of presents, including a capital pony, and I took my leave as before. His last words were :- "I may see you in Peking in the 8th moon ", [September-October]

In the course of our conversation the Tale Lama referred to the resoluteness of his country and the fact that it had no friends abroad. I replied that he was mistaken, that he and Tibet had many well-wishers in America and in other countries, who hoped to see him and his people prosperous and happy. I

-10-

said that it was my intention to report to you the substance of our conversation and that I hoped that, should I be so fortunate as to see him again in Peking, I might be able to give him a message from you confirming what I had said.

Altogether it was a most novel and interesting experience. The Tale Lama seems to me a man of undoubted intelligence, open-minded, perhaps as the result of his misfortunes of the last four years, a very agreeable, kindly, thoughtful host, and a personage of great dignity, though simple withal, quick-tempered, perhaps, but of a cheerful temperament.

There is much more I could say of this trip but I fear I have, in my gratification over it, said too much already. I felt a deeper and more complete satisfaction with these two interviews with the mysterious potentate and incarnation of the god Chenrezig than would any one who had not, like myself, given so many years of their life to Tibet. To be

当面感谢他对我的善意和好感。特使说，达赖喇嘛一定会很高兴见到我。他极力敦促我尽快启程。

On the 13th of this month, there being no pressing work in the legation, I set out with a couple of mule litters and a mule pack train and in five days, across the Chihli plain and the mountains to the west of it, I came to Wu-t'ai shan, where I had been once before, —some twenty-three years ago.

这个月 13 号，公使馆事务不忙，我就坐着骡子拉的轿子出发了，还带着骡子驮队。我们花了五天的时间，穿过了直隶平原和山区，来到了山西的西面，最终到了五台山。实际上我过去也去过那里，不过那是在二十三年前了。

The day after my arrival my friend, the lama agent of the Tale Lama, met me there and at once arranged for my reception by His Holiness for the next day (19th of June). The temple in which the Tale Lama is staying is on the top of a rather high and precipitous hill and a long flight of marble steps to leads up to it. At the top of the steps is the gate to the temple; here I found the Tale Lama's body guard, armed with rough Martini rifles made in Lhasa, drawn up on one side of the path leading from the gate to a small pavilion covered with blue tiles, and on the other the Chinese guard sent to protect him by the Government during his stay at the Wu-t'ai shan. A large number of Tibetan officials, lamas and laymen, were waiting at the gate for me, and a couple of them arranged in my hands the ceremonial scarf (katag, in Tibetan), which is customary for guests to present to their hosts, and a very large one of which I had brought with me.

我们到达目的地的第二天，我那位达赖喇嘛特使朋友已经在那里迎接我了，很快就安排我第二天（6月19号）拜见尊贵的喇嘛。达赖喇嘛居住的寺庙在一座山高坡陡的峰顶子上。山下有一条长长的大理石台阶通往上面。台阶最顶层就是庙门。在那里，我见到了达赖喇嘛的贴身护卫。他们都配有拉萨造的粗制马提尼步枪。这些贴身护卫整齐地站在通往大门的道路一侧。这条小路通向一座蓝瓦的小亭子。在道路的另一侧，则站着汉族护卫。在喇嘛停驻五台山期间，朝廷派这些人前来护卫。很多西藏官员都在大门

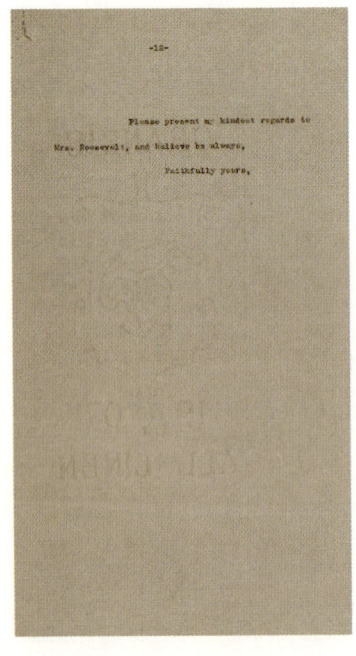

处等着我。这当中有喇嘛，也有非宗教人士。其中一些人向我进献了哈达（藏语中指作为礼仪用的丝织品）。而按照惯例，客人们也应该向主人们进献哈达。也就是由于这个原因，我也随身携带了一方很大、很长的哈达。

I was then led by two lamas to the pavilion in which the Tale Lama was to receive me, a small building with two rooms and a corridor between them. A yellow silk curtain hung before the door of the room to the right; this was raised and I saw the Tale Lama seated in an arm chair on a slightly raised platform. His appearance took me absolutely by surprise. I had imagined a rather ascetic looking youth, bent by constantly sitting bow-legged on cushions, with a sallow complexion and a far-away meditative look. On the contrary I found a man of thirty-three, with a very bright face, rather dark brown, a moustache and a small tuft of hair under his lower lip. His eyes were large, rather prominent and obliquely set; his eyebrows rising slightly towards the temples gave him a rather narquois expression. His mouth was large; his teeth were white and perfect. His head was bare and as it had not been shaved for some days, it added to the general worldliness of his appearance. He was dressed in an Imperial yellow satin gown and the shawl which all lamas wear and which hangs over the left shoulder and passes around the body, was of bright vermillion silk. His boots were yellow with blue braiding. His ears were large, but well-shaped; his hands good and thin.

接着，两位喇嘛引着我走到亭子那里。达赖喇嘛即将在那里接见我。那个亭子很小，有两间房，中间由走廊相连。右侧房间的门上挂着一个黄色的绸缎帘。门帘揭开，我终于目睹了达赖喇嘛的尊容。在一个略高于地面的平台上，他稳坐在一把扶手椅里。他的相貌可着实让我吃了一惊。我曾经想象，这位喇嘛应该是一位看起来很年轻的禁欲人士，由于常年盘坐在拜垫上身体会变得很弯。他的气色也不会太好。我猜他的眼神会朝向远方，沉思着什么。可是，恰恰相反，我面前的这个人三十三岁，红光满面。他的皮肤呈深棕色，长着胡子，下巴上还蓄着一小撮毛儿。他长着一对大眼睛，目光如炬，只是有点斜。他的眉毛朝寺庙方向轻微扬起，带着一丝轻微的鄙夷和嘲讽神气。他的嘴巴很大，牙齿洁白，很强健。他头上光秃秃的，有些天没剃头了，这让他看起来更世故了。他身上穿着皇家绸缎黄袍，左肩上裹着所有喇嘛都披着的大披巾，斜向下一直裹住身体。披巾由鲜红色的丝绸制成。他脚穿一双黄靴子，靴子上还带着蓝穗子。他长着一对儿外形很好看的大耳朵，双手很瘦、保养得很好。

I stood before him, bowed, and placed the scarf I had in my hands at his feet and he put the one he held in my out-stretched hands. Then I took off my hat and was asked to sit in an armchair placed in front of him. The only persons present were two attendants, an abbot who acted as interpreter, and Mr. Haskins of our Legation, who accompanied me.

我站在他面前，鞠躬行礼，将手中拿着的哈达放到他脚下。他也把他手中拿的哈达放到我伸出的双手中。然后，我摘下帽子，奉命坐在他面前摆放的一把扶手椅中。在这次会面中，在场的除我们之外只有两个随从。一位是担任翻译的住持，还有一位是公使馆里和我做伴儿来此的哈斯金斯先生。

An attendant brought in a cup of tea for the Tale Lama, who touched it to his lips; then a cup was brought for me and placed on a little table beside me. After a while a bowl of sweetened rice was brought him and then one to me. Then a low table was placed before me with cakes, dried fruits, sweets, etc., on it.

一个随从给达赖喇嘛递上一杯茶。喇嘛只是呷了一口，抿了抿嘴唇。随从也给我上了一杯茶，放在我身旁的小桌子上。过了一会儿，他又给我和喇嘛各上了一碗糯米饭。随后，随从在我面前又放了一张低矮的桌子，摆上蛋糕、果脯和糖果等小吃。

The Tale Lama first asked me a number of questions concerning my journey from Peking, my ago, how long I had been in China, etc. He spoke very low to the abbot who stood before him, and he in turn repeated in Chinese what His Holiness had said.

达赖喇嘛先问了我几个问题，例如：我从北京到五台山这一路上的旅途、我的年龄、我在中国待了多久等等。他先用很低的声音，对方丈说话，然后方丈又把他的话翻译成汉语说给我听。

After that he said that he had heard much about me and was most pleased to see me. He especially alluded to the fact that he had heard it said that I spoke his language. I replied to him in Tibetan this time and much to his satisfaction, as his eyes brightened and he gave a smile which showed all his teeth. After about a half hour's conversation he said that this was my first and formal visit to him, but that he hoped that I could remain at the Wu-t'ai shan a few days longer, so that he could see me again. I said that I would await his pleasure.

之后，喇嘛说他对我已经是久仰"大名"了，见到我极为高兴。他还特别指出，他听说我能讲他的语言。这次我用藏语回答了他。他看起来很满意，因为我看到，他双眼放光，冲着我微笑，牙齿全露了出来。大约谈了半个小时之后，他说虽然这是我第一次正式拜见他，但他还是希望我能在五台山多待几天。这样，他还能再次见到我。我回答说，我会恭候他的召唤。

On the 21st I was again received by the Tale Lama, with the same simple ceremonial, and I had an hour and a half conversation with him. He asked me what I thought of the relations of India with Tibet, of the trade convention recently concluded concerning Tibet, of the proposed visit of the Panchen rinpoche lama to Peking, etc., etc. ... He thought that it would be a good thing for him to go to Peking to see the Emperor, but he did not know yet whether he would go or not...

21 号那天，我再次承蒙达赖喇嘛的召见。这次的仪式仍旧与上次相同，很简单。我和他谈了一个半小时。他询问我对印度与西藏关系的看法，觉得最近缔结的有关西藏的贸易协定怎么样，对班禅活佛拟访问北京的事项怎么看，等等。……他认为自己应该去北京觐见皇帝，但拿不准自己该不该去。

After talking over at considerable length a variety of questions concerning Tibet, with which I will not bother you, he said again that he had been most pleased to meet me and that he knew that I was a friend of Tibet and the Tibetans and that he wished to have a friend whose opinion he could ask when necessary; he had heard that I had done well as Minister at Peking and he would be much pleased if I would, whenever I saw fit, write to him, and he would do likewise with me. I told him I would be much honored, but that as I held an official position in Peking, he would understand that certain limitations were imposed upon me and that I could only do certain things to oblige him. This he said he thoroughly understood and said that I could talk to his agents at Peking as to himself and that it would be correctly reported to him.

我们花了很长一段时间，谈论西藏事务。不过，在这里我就不说那些来打扰您了。喇嘛又说，他见到我非常高兴，还说他知道我是西藏的朋友，也是西藏人的朋友。而且，他也希望在必要的时候，自己能有个朋友征求意见。他说，听说我在北京做大使时工作很出色，因此如果我能在合适的时候给他写信，他会非常高兴。同样，他也会给我写信。我告诉他自己深感荣幸。不过由于我在北京担任公职，因此希望他能理解我有时会受到很多限制，只能在某些方面帮他的忙。关于这一点，他表示完全理解，还说，回到北京我还可以和他的特使们会谈，就像和他本人会谈一样。会谈的内容会如实地汇报给他。

He then asked me if I had the photograph of "My Emperor". I said

I had at Peking and he requested that I send it to him. This I am doing to-day.

接着他又问我是否有"我皇帝陛下"的照片。我说我有照片，只是放在北京了。他请求我把照片寄给他。我今天就会寄。

The Tale Lama then gave me a gilt image of the Buddha and a large ceremonial scarf to present to you from him, after which he gave me a number of presents, including a capital pony, and I took my leave as before. His last words were: "I may see you in Peking in the 8th moon", (September-October)

达赖喇嘛接着给我一尊镀金的佛像，还让我向您转交一方哈达。而后，他又给了我一些礼物，其中还有匹小马。随后，我就像上次一样告退了。我还记得他最后说的话是："也许在阴历八月，我能在北京见到你。"他说的时间，指的是公历的九十月份。

In the course of our conversation the Tale Lama referred to the remoteness of his country and the fact that it had no friends abroad. I replied that he was mistaken, that he and Tibet had many well-wishers in America and in other countries, who hoped to see him and his people prosperous and happy. I said that it was my intention to report to you the substance of our conversation and that I hoped that, should I be so fortunate as to see him again in Peking, I might be able to give him a message from you confirming what I had said.

在我们交谈的过程中，达赖喇嘛曾提到自己的家乡西藏山高水远、地处偏僻，没有什么外国朋友。我回答说，他说错了。因为在美国和很多别的国家，都有很多人在为他和西藏祈福，都希望他的人民富强、幸福。我也对他说，我已经打算向您汇报我们的会谈内容，也希望如果我有幸能在北京再次见到他，能给他捎去您的口信儿，让他知道我确实向您汇报过这些事。

Altogether it was a most novel and interesting experience. The Tale

Lama seems to me a man of undoubted intelligence, open-minded, perhaps as the result of his misfortunes of the last four years, a very agreeable, kindly, thoughtful host, and a personage of great dignity, though simple withal, quick-tempered, perhaps, but of a cheerful temperament.

总的来说，这真是新奇有趣的经历。在我看来，达赖喇嘛这个人无疑很聪明，思想也开放。也许是由于过去四年的不幸经历，他和蔼可亲、善良慈祥、周到体贴。而且，他很有尊严，虽然头脑有些简单，脾气有点儿急躁，但性情却开朗活泼。

There is much more I could say of this trip but I fear I have, in my gratification over it, said too much already. I felt a deeper and more complete satisfaction with these two interviews with the mysterious potentate and incarnation of the god Shenrezig than would anyone who had not, like myself, given so many years of their life to Tibet. To be seated talking familiarly with the Tale Lama, with one of his abbots standing behind me, with His Holiness fly-flapper keeping the flies off my head, and he seeing that my tea cup was kept filled with hot tea, asking me to open a correspondence with him, to be his counselor and friend; it was all too extraordinary. I could not believe my ears and eyes.

关于这次旅行，我还有很多想说的。但是，我害怕我已经在得意忘形之下说了太多惹您烦了。我觉得，如果不像我一样，曾在西藏生活过多年，那么任何人都不会在与西藏这位神奇统治者、这位仙乃日神的转世活佛的会谈中获得如此深刻和完全的满足感。想一想：我坐着和达赖喇嘛亲密会谈；他的一位住持站在我身后，手拿着尊贵喇嘛的苍蝇拍为我驱赶蚊蝇；他要随从随时给我的茶杯斟满热茶；他要我和他通信；他希望我成为他的顾问和朋友——这一切都是多么神奇、多么不同寻常啊！我甚至都不敢相信自己的双耳和双眼。

I am sending you in a box the image of the Buddha and the big white silk katag the Tale Lama directed me to offer to you in his name. I hope

I have not bored you, but you have always been so sympathetic with my work that I thought you would like to hear of this unique experience, for, though the Tale Lama has in the last few years seen several Russians, the receptions have, I think, been more or less formal and brief.

我随信给您寄去了一尊佛像和达赖喇嘛让我转交给您的一方长长的白色丝绸哈达，都放在了盒子里。希望我的信没惹您烦。不过一直以来，您对我的工作都感同身受，所以我想您可能也愿意听听我这次非凡的经历。因为虽然达赖喇嘛在过去几年里见过几个俄国人，但我觉得他接待那些人的时候或多或少都较为拘谨，时间也较短。

Let me most heartily congratulate you on the success so far of Mr. Taft. I feel convinced that he will be elected with the same unanimity as he was nominated.

Please present my kindest regards to Mrs. Roosevelt, and believe be always,

Faithfully yours,

Rockhill

请允许我向您表达我最衷心的祝贺！到目前为止，塔夫脱先生一直都很成功。他已经获得了全体提名，我相信他肯定也会全票当选。

请向罗斯福夫人转达我最真诚、最良好的问候。

您真诚的柔克义，敬上

信二

AMERICAN LEGATION,
PEKING, CHINA
November 8, 1908
中国，北京，美国驻中国北京
公使馆，1908 年 11 月 8 日

Dear Mr. President:
尊敬的总统先生：

I have deferred replying sooner to your very kind letters of August 1st and September 7th, so as to be able to give you the information you express the wish to have concerning, "What passes between the Dalai Lama and the Chinese Government during his stay at Peking". Although he has not left yet, the story can already be told; his case is already settled.

抱歉，我没能按时回复您 8 月 1 号和 9 月 7 号的来信，因此也就没能向您提供所需信息——"达赖喇嘛在驻留北京期间与大清政府的关系"。虽然喇嘛现在仍在北京，但我还是可以向您汇报这一事件。他的事已经板上钉钉了。

After much hesitation, with much

misgiving, and only after repeated and peremptory representations from Peking, the Dalai Lama and his suite left the Wu-tai shan, where I had seen him in June, in the latter part of September and travelled to a place called Tingchou on the railway between here and Hankow. There he found a special train waiting for him, and, on September 28th, he made his entry into Peking, where he was received with the highest honors. He took up his residence at the big lamasery outside the north gates of the city.

......

在北京多次强制要求下，经过一番犹豫，满心怀着担忧和疑虑，达赖喇嘛及其一行离开了五台山。您还记得吗？我 6 月曾在那里见过他。9 月末，他们来到一个叫定州的地方。那个地方就在北京和汉口的铁路沿线上。9 月 28 号，那里有一列专门等候他的火车。他乘坐火车来到北京，受到了最高的礼遇和接待。他在北京北城门外最大的喇嘛庙藏传佛教寺庙黄寺安顿下来。……

The day after his arrival in Peking the Dalai Lama sent one of his officers

Indian Government to be a Russian agent and his presence in Tibet was one of the direct causes of the British expedition of 1904), had been to see him by order of the Dalai Lama to ask information concerning the settlement of Tibetan affairs the Chinese Government proposed to make, and of which he was absolutely in the dark. He also wished the Russian Minister's services: should the Dalai Lama remain here and settle them, or should he return to Tibet at once?

Mr. Korostovets said he had told Dorjieff that he thought the Dalai Lama had only to submit to what the Chinese Government might decide upon, but he had no advice to give. The time when Russia was concerned in advising or supporting eastern rulers was at and; as a spiritual ruler Russia was greatly interested in the welfare of the Dalai Lama, as a temporal ruler he must obey China.

Dorjieff

Dorjieff then had said that, since Russia would not advise the Dalai Lama, he must ask the British Minister to assist him. Mr. Korostovets told him he thought it would be quite useless, as Sir John Jordan had told him that he could hold no direct relations with the Tibetans; so far as he was concerned, questions concerning Tibet must be settled with the Chinese Government, the suzerain state. The Russian Minister then advised Dorjieff to see me, the representative of an absolutely disinterested power and ask my advice. This Dorjieff said he would be pleased to do, if the Russian Minister would arrange an interview. I told Mr. Korostovets that I would be pleased to see Dorjieff whenever he called.

On the 21st Dorjieff called on me, accompanied by another Khampo, a confidential advisor of the Dalai Lama. Dorjieff was a few years ago a terribly important figure in the eyes of the Indian Government, a deep and designing personage, intriguing

to see me, to ask concerning my health and requesting me to come and see him. I suggested that he wait until after his audience; as soon, however, as it was put off he sent again and asked me to come to his residence. He allowed me to bring all the staff of the Legation to present to him. I saw him on October 6th, the day he should have had his audience. ... My reception, at which no Chinese were present, only lasted some ten minutes. He asked after you and whether you had received his greetings sent you from the Wu-tai shan. I told him you had and that you had directed me to tell him that you were greatly pleased at receiving them and that you wished him all happiness and prosperity. He said he would send some of his abbots in a day or two to see me.

在来到北京的第二天，达赖喇嘛就派自己的一位官员来见我，问我身体怎么样，还邀请我来与他会晤。我建议他等到觐见光绪帝和慈禧太后以后再邀请我去。可是事与愿违，面圣事宜一再推迟，他于是再次派人邀请我去他的驻地。他还允许我带上公使馆的所有人员去见他。10 月 6 号那天，我见到了喇嘛。原本那天，他应该觐见皇帝的。……这次的会面没有一个中国人在场，只持续了大约十分钟。他向我问起您，还询问您是否收到了前次来自五台山的问候。我告诉他您已经收到，还转告他，您收到他的祝福十分高兴，也祝福他幸福、安康。他说，在最近一两天，他还会派自己的住持来见我。

On October 9th the Chinese Foreign Office informed the Legations that the Dalai Lama would receive the Foreign Representatives and their suites any day from noon to 3 o'clock, Sundays excepted, when they would be presented to him by certain Chinese officials deputed for that purpose...

10月9号，大清外务部公所告知美国驻京公使馆，除周日以外，每天从中午到下午三时，达赖喇嘛都可以接见外国代表及其随行人员。专门负责此事的中国官员会为达赖喇嘛引见各国代表。……

On October 19th the Russian Minister called on me and said that the Dalai Lama's Councillor, Khanpo Nawang lozang dorja, better known

Tibet, the dividing of the country into regular administrative districts as in China proper, the reorganization of the military forces of the country, of the currency, of education, the extension of agriculture and stock-raising, and of the opening of roads, etc. If these were really the reforms contemplated I could not see what objection the Dalai Lama could have to them. Furthermore, military questions, relations with foreign states, educational questions (in some countries) were all imperial matters which could not be left to the various states to deal with independently.

Dorjieff said the Dalai Lama had absolutely no objection to raise against the extension of education in Tibet nor to military reforms. He was also perfectly satisfied with the treaty concluded with Tibet and China by Great Britain and with the recent regulations for trade between Tibet and India. He had no fault to find with the existing relations with Russia; he solely feared China's encroachment on his Temporal authority.

He wished to place before the Emperor two points which he considered of paramount importance. The first one that the Yellow Church should be maintained in all its honors, the second that the right should be given him to submit directly to the Throne any memorials he might wish to make, after previous arrangement with the Chinese Amban (i. e., Minister Resident) in Lhasa and without passing as at present through the hands of the Viceroy of Sech'uan and the Li-fan Pu (Board of Dependencies), either of which might pigeon-hole them. All other questions he considered of minor importance as compared to these.

I said concerning the first point to which the Pontiff attached importance, that I felt convinced that the Emperor and His Government would do nothing whatsoever to lessen the dignity of the Yellow Church, that it was the traditional policy of this dynasty to uphold it; I thought he might confidently count as a continuance of the Imperial favor. Concerning the second point, I advised

by his Russified name of Dorjieff, (he is a Russian subject and was once supposed by the Indian Government to be a Russian agent, and his presence in Tibet was one of the direct causes of the British expedition of 1904), had been to see him by order of the Dalai Lama to ask information concerning the settlement of Tibetan affairs the Chinese Government proposed to make, and of which he was absolutely in the dark. He also wished the Russian Minister's advice: should the Dalai Lama remain here and settle them, or should he return to Tibet at once?

10 月 19 号，俄国大使来拜访我，说达赖喇嘛的顾问堪布·阿旺·洛桑多吉（他的俄语名字更有名——德尔智，是一位俄国人，曾经被印度政府认为是俄国代表。他在西藏的存在成为 1904 年英国远征西藏的直接原因之一）奉达赖喇嘛之命前来见他，咨询清政府拟解决西藏事件的方案，因为关于这一点达赖喇嘛一无所知。德尔智还希望就达赖喇嘛应留在北京，与清政府商谈藏务，还是应立即返回西藏这一问题，征求俄国大使的意见。

Mr. Korostovetz said he had told

Dorjieff that he thought the Dalai Lama had only to submit to what the Chinese Government might decide upon, but he had no advice to give. The time when Russian was concerned in advising or supporting eastern rulers was at an end; as a spiritual ruler Russian was greatly interested in the welfare of the Dalai Lama, as a temporal ruler he must obey China.

　　俄国大使廓索维慈先生说，他告诉德尔智，达赖喇嘛应该服从清政府的决定，除此以外他别无建议。作为精神领袖的达赖喇嘛，俄国人对他的福祉倍感兴趣，但作为世俗领袖，他就必须服从中国中央政府。

　　Dorjieff then had said that, since Russia would not advice the Dalai Lama, he must ask the British Minister to assist him. Mr. Korostovetz told him he thought it would be quite useless, as Sir John Jordan had told him that he could hold no direct relations with the Tibetans; so far as he was concerned, questions concerning Tibet must be settled with the Chinese Government, the suzerain state. The Russian Minister then advised Dorjieff to see me, the representative of an absolutely disinterested power and ask my

101

advice. This Dorjieff said he would be pleased to do, if the Russian Minister would arrange an interview. I told Mr. Korostovetz that I would be pleased to see Dorjieff whenever he called.

然后德尔智说，既然俄国无法为达赖喇嘛提出建议，他就得请英国驻华公使朱尔典爵士帮忙。廓索维慈先生回答说，他不能与藏人直接联系，据他所知，涉及西藏的问题应和中国政府商议解决。俄国大使也因此建议德尔智来见我，征求我的意见，因为我所代表的国家在这一系列事件中是绝对中立的。关于这一点，德尔智说如果俄国大使能安排会面，他将十分乐意前来见我。我告诉廓索维慈大使，无论何时，我都很高兴与德尔智会面。

On the 21st Dorjieff called on me, accompanied by another Khampo, a confidential advisor of the Dalai Lama. Dorjieff was a few years ago a terribly important figure in the eyes of the Indian Government, a deep and designing personage, intriguing in Tibet in the sole interest of Russia.

21号，德尔智来拜访我。和他一道的还有另一位堪布（即住持之意），也是达赖喇嘛的心腹顾问。几年前，

德尔智在印度政府眼中是一个极其重
要的人物。印度政府认为，他富于心
计、诡计多端、令人难以捉摸，介入
西藏事件只是为了俄国的利益。

I found him a very quiet, well-mannered man, impressionable like all Mongols, and apparently, but very little less ignorant of politics and the world in general than the Tibetans, though he has travelled over Europe and Asia. He is evidently devoted to his religion and to the Head of his Church, the Dalai Lama, whom he has sought to assist as best he could. It was natural for him to turn to Russia for advice, being a Russian subject and having received his early education in that country, but I do not think he was or is more of an intriguer than any Asiatic would be when confronted for the first time with, to him, such a new and intricate question as Tibet's policy in Central Asian politics and in relation to the two great empires its neighbors.

不过通过这次会面，我却发现他
为人十分安静、彬彬有礼，像所有的
蒙古人一样敏感，而且很显然，尽管
曾游历欧洲和亚洲，但他对于政治和

be in store for my friend the Dalai Lama, 77th-13th again's, if not for China.

It seems to me that it was a great pity that the British Government did not secure the right to station a trade officer at Lhasa when it was negotiating the regulations for trade between India and Tibet. His presence there would have a restraining influence on the Chinese and Tibetans and might otherwise assist in a powerful change in the administration of the country and prevent occurrences which may again undanger British interests in that country. Of course Russia would have asked for the same privilege, but I can see no reason against her having it one way in favor of it, especially since Great Britain and Russia have already concluded an agreement concerning Tibet. This, however, is none of my business, though it interests me greatly. The special interest to me is in that I have probably been a witness to the overthrow of the temporal power of the head of the

Yellow

Yellow Church, which, curiously enough, I heard twenty years ago predicted in Tibet, where it was commonly said that the thirteenth Dalai Lama would be the last and my client in the thirteenth.

I have told both the British Minister and the Russian of the substance of all my conversations with the Dalai Lama's counsellors and of the conclusions I have reached concerning him and his pretensions. I think they both agree with me in my views.

This curious episode, this glimpse into pure Asiatic politics, seems to me of peculiar interest. I hope you will think likewise and pardon the length of my narrative.

Always faithfully yours,

世界事务的了解并不比普通的西藏人多。很显然，他虔诚地献身于自己的宗教信仰，忠实于自己的教会领袖达赖喇嘛。而且，他一直以来都在尽自己的最大努力帮助喇嘛。他转向俄国寻求帮助原本是很自然的，因为他是俄国人，早年也是在俄国接受教育。但我认为，在初次面临西藏在中亚政局的策略及其与周边两个大国之间关系这类复杂的新问题时，他在过去或者说现在所做的一切也并不比任何一个亚洲人在这种情况下有可能表现得更为狡猾。

Dorjieff told me that the Dalai Lama had heard said that the Chinese Government was making certain important changes in the internal administration of Tibet. He did not know their nature and extent. He wished to know whether in my opinion, it were better for him to remain in Peking until the changes were made or return at once to Lhasa. He was without any of his advisors on temporal matters; he felt unable to cope with the questions which might be raised without their assistance, but he feared to go until the program of Tibetan reforms had been settled, for he apprehended that the Chinese Government sought to curtail power he and his predecessors had wielded from before the Manchus came to the Throne of China.

德尔智告诉我，达赖喇嘛听说清政府在西藏内政事务方面正在制定某些重大改革举措。但喇嘛却并不知道这些改革的实质和程度。他希望征求我的意见：究竟他是应该留在北京等候这些改革举措的实施，还是应立刻返回拉萨？在世俗事务方面，他没有任何顾问。没有顾问们的帮助，他觉得自己无法应对这些问题。不过，他认为自己应等到西藏改革举措确定后，再返回拉萨。因为他十分担心，他和前任们在满族入统中原之前在西藏行使的权力会被清政府削弱。

... I understood from the Chinese public press that the Government contemplated an administrative reform of Tibet, the dividing of the country into regular administrative districts as in China proper, the reorganization of the military forces of the country, of the currency, of education, the extension or agriculture and stock-raising, and of the opening of roads, etc. If these were really the reforms contemplated, I could not see what objection the Dalai Lama could have to them. Furthermore, military questions, relations with foreign states, educational questions (in some countries) were all imperial matters which could not be left to the various states to deal with independently.

……我从中国的新闻报纸上了解到清政府正在酝酿有关西藏的行政改革，包括将西藏划分为与中国内地相同的行政区划，重新组建西藏的军事力量，改革财政、教育，发展农牧业以及修建道路等。如果这真是计划中的改革内容，我看不到达赖喇嘛反对这项改革的任何理由。不仅如此，军事、外交和教育问题（在某些地区）都是皇家中央的分内之事，不应该留给各个省份去单独处理。

Dorjieff said the Dalai Lama had absolutely no objection to raise against the extension of education in Tibet nor to military reforms... He had no fault to find with the existing relations with Russia; he solely feared China's encroachment on his temporal authority. He wished to place before the Emperor two points which he considered of paramount importance. The first was that the Yellow Church should be maintained in all its honors, the second that the right should be given him to submit directly to the Throne any memorials he might wish to make, after previous arrangement with the Chinese Amban (i. e., Minister Resident) in Lhasa, and without passing as at present through the hands of the Viceroy of Szech'uan and Li-fan Pu (Board of Dependencies), either of which might pigeon-hole them. All other questions he considered of minor importance as compared to them.

德尔智说，达赖喇嘛绝不反对在西藏扩大教育，也不反对军事改革。他认为目前西藏与俄国的关系也没什么问题。他只是害怕清政府会侵犯他的世俗权威。他希望向清政府提出两个他认为至关重要的问题。第一，黄教（藏传佛教格鲁派的俗称）应该得到保留和最尊贵、最崇高的推崇。第二，在与拉萨的驻藏大臣（即常驻公使）协商好之后，他应该有权直接向朝廷呈送奏折、上书言事，而不需要像现在一样还得通过四川总督和理藩部之手。"西藏事务重大，事事通过驻藏大臣每多误事，今后凡遇大事，可否直接自行具奏……"因为这两个部门都有可能将其奏折搁置下来，置之不理。他认为，和这两个问题相比，其他问题都不那么重要。

I said concerning the first point to which the Pontiff attached importance, that I felt convinced that the Emperor and His Government would do nothing whatsoever to lessen the dignity of the Yellow Church, that it was the traditional policy of his dynasty to uphold it; I thought he might confidently count on a continuance of the Imperial Favor. Concerning the second point, I advised the Dalai Lama to ascertain informally how such a request would be received and act accordingly. Personally I thought what he asked for was reasonable and in the interest of good government, that it insured his representations reaching the Throne and that I could not see what serious objections could be made to it if the Chinese Government was made aware how greatly he desired this privileges.

我确信，皇帝和他的政府绝不会做任何贬低黄教声誉的事，这也是该王朝一贯所持的传统政策。我认为他（指达赖喇嘛）很可能满怀信心地指望能继续获得帝国的支持。关于第二点，我建议达赖喇嘛非正式地了解一下，这样的要求怎样才能被转递到皇帝手中并被恰当处理。我个人认为他的要求是合理的，对于政府的良好运作也是有益的，可以保证他的代表能直接与皇帝接触。如果清政府意识到达赖喇嘛对于这项特权是多么渴望，我认为他们不会严重反对此事。

Dorjieff said that he would report at once to the Dalai Lama what I had said and that he would bring me a draft of what he wished to place before the Emperor concerning the two points mentioned above. He said that could these be settled the Dalai Lama would at once leave for Lhasa; all other questions could be arranged by some of his abbots whom he would leave here to discuss them with the Board of Dependencies.

德尔智说他会立刻向达赖喇嘛汇报我的回复，还说会给我带来一份草稿，陈述他希望如何就上述两点向清政府进折。他说，如果这些问题得到了解决，达赖喇嘛将会立刻动身返回拉萨。所有其他问题都可以由喇嘛的一些住持安排。这些堪布喇嘛将会留在北京，继续与理藩部探讨解决方案。

I said that I had for the last three years constantly advised the Dalai Lama to return without delay to Lhasa, and that I still thought this highly desirable. He should, however, show the Chinese Government that he was sincerely favorable to all measures for the good of his country, as on this must depend the continuance of the Imperial favor and the granting to him of the favors he so much desired.

过去三年来，我一直建议达赖喇嘛尽早返回拉萨，勿要迟疑。现在我仍然认为这是上策。然而，他应向中国政府表明，他本人是发自内心地支持清廷在西藏采取的各项利于西藏的举措，因为他能否继续得到清廷的支持，以及清廷是否能给予他所期望的支持，完全取决于此。

I gathered from this very long conversation that the Dalai Lama cared very little, if at all, for anything which did not affect his personal privileges and prerogatives, that he separated entirely his cause from that of the people of Tibet, which he was willing to abandon entirely to the mercy of China. He did not care particularly concerning the contemplated administrative reforms, so long as he could feel assured that his personal honors and privileges were safe and, if possible, slightly added to. The Chinese Government must have reached the same conclusion. While it has treated him simply as the head of the Yellow Church and has shown him honors accordingly, it has made him clearly realize that he was a Subject of the Emperor...

从这次长时间的谈话，我得出（如下）结论：凡不影响他个人特权的事情，他几乎都不会在意；他将自己的事业与西藏人民的事业区分得泾渭分明，他愿意将西藏人民的事业完全交由清廷任意处置。只要他觉得他的个人荣誉和特权能有所保障，如有可能还可增加的话，他就不会特别在意（清廷）打算在西藏进行的行政改革。清政府一定也得出了同样的结论。虽然清廷仅仅将他视作黄教首领，也予以他相应的尊重，但这都让他清楚地意识到：他是皇帝的臣民。……

The title of Prince of the First Order has been conferred upon him, and on October 30th an Imperial banquet was given him, at which the Emperor was present, and many rich presents have been sent him by the Empress Dowager and the Emperor.

达赖喇嘛被授予了第一等爵（和硕亲王）的头衔。10 月 30 号，大清朝廷摆出御膳满汉全席宴请他。光绪皇帝本人出席了宴会。皇帝和皇太后慈禧太后还赏赐给他很多珍稀礼物。

On November 3rd the Empress Dowager celebrated with great ceremony her seventy-fifth birthday. The Dalai Lama with the princess and Ministers of State offered her congratulations. The same day appeared an edict in the name of the Empress Dowager conferring a new title on the Dalai Lama, longer by four characters than that he had formerly borne, granting him an annual pension of ten Thousand taels, but also ordering him to start at once for Tibet and enjoining on him to induce his people to obey the laws and keep the peace, and on his personally to comply with the laws and show his gratitude to the Throne for protecting the Yellow Church and undertaking to insure peace to Tibet. ...

11 月 3 日，慈禧太后大摆筵席，庆祝自己七十五岁生日。达赖喇嘛和国务大臣都为她送去了祝福。同一天，慈禧太后以自己的名义下诏，为达赖喇嘛册封。这个新头衔比之前的还多了四个汉字。达赖喇嘛业经循照旧制封为"西天大善自在佛"，兹特加封为"诚顺赞化西天大善自在佛"。此外，他每年还将获得一万两银子的俸禄。同时，清政府还命令他立刻动身返回西藏，劝诚西藏人民要遵守法律，维护当地的和平稳定。另外，清政府还要求他个人也要遵守法律，对朝廷保护黄教、保证西藏地区和平等举措要满怀感激之情。……

On November 5th the Dalai Lama sent again in great haste to consult me; he was in a terrible dilemma. He had been told that he should submit at once a memorial to the Throne thanking it for the imperial edict of the 3rd. The terms in which he was to express his thanks had been dedicated to him and he was told not a word could be added to the draft. He was ready to thank the Empress Dowager for the honors conferred on him, but he could not bring himself to thank her for having stated that he should not have the right to memorialize the Throne jointly with the Amban, one privilege he had most desired.

11月5日，达赖喇嘛又匆匆遣人请教我的意见。他说自己进退两难。因为他被告知应立刻向朝廷呈送一份奏折，感谢3日那天慈禧太后的诏书。他表达谢意需要使用的用语和措辞也都已经呈送给他。他必须严格按照这个草本，一个字也不能增加。其实他早已准备好了感谢慈禧太后授予自己头衔，但他无法强迫自己"感谢"慈禧太后剥夺了他与驻藏大臣一道直接上书皇帝的权利。因为这是他最希望获得的特权之一。

His messenger showed me a draft of what the Dalai Lama wished to include in his memorial of thanks, (I enclose copy of this rough draft), but the only satisfaction he had got was being told that if he wished to submit these remarks to the Throne, he must put it in a special memorial which should be handed to Board of Dependencies for submission, but no promise was made that it would be submitted to the Empress Dowager.

达赖喇嘛的信使给我看了他希望在上表奏折中加上的一份草本（随信我给您寄去了这份粗略的草稿）。他唯一能够确认的是，他被告知，如果他希望向皇帝上陈这些话，就必须将其写入一份特殊奏折。这份奏折应先上呈理藩部。不过，理藩部可不能保证会将其上呈慈禧太后。

I said that I saw absolutely no way out of the difficulty; the Dalai Lama must submit to his sovereign's command. He had received many honors, his relations with India had been satisfactorily arranged by China, the interests of the Yellow Church were safe. He must take the bitter with the sweet, and the only suggestion I could make that he should not delay too long complying with the wishes of the Chinese Government, as it might be misunderstood and lead to further complications.

看起来没有办法解决这个难题，达赖喇嘛必须服从其君主的命令。他已经得到了很多荣誉封号，与印度的关系也得到了清政府的满意安排，黄教的利益也得以保全。在得到好处的同时也必须做出让步，我对他唯一的建议，就是不要再犹豫迟疑，立即答应清政府的要求，否则将引起误解并导致事态进一步趋向复杂。

The messenger said the Dalai Lama realized the difficulty of his situation, he did not think there was any way out but compliance with the orders of the government, but as he had consulted me freely since we had first met, he deemed it proper to submit also this matter to my judgment.

信使说达赖喇嘛已经意识到自己困难的处境。他知道除了遵照朝廷旨意，自己别无选择。但既然在我二人首次会面时他就曾自由地征求我的意见，此次关于这件事他认为也应该请我判断一下。

Yesterday one of the abbots was here to see me; he said the memorial of thanks had not yet been sealed by Dalai, but I gathered that it would be in a day or so, and with that the whole question will be closed for the time being.

昨天，喇嘛的一位住持来这里见我。他说，喇嘛还没有在感谢皇帝陛下的奏折上盖章。但我想，也就在这一两天了。此事一结，整个问题暂时就会告一段落了。

The Dalai Lama will probably start on his journey back to Lhasa about the end of the month and reach his capital by May of next year.

……

这月末达赖喇嘛可能就会启程返回拉萨。他明年 5 月之前就会回到自己的地盘了。

……

I have told both the British Minister and the Russian of the substance of all my conversations with the Dalai Lama's councilors and of the conclusions I have reached concerning him and his pretensions. I think they both agree with me in my views.

我将我与德尔智及喇嘛顾问们所有谈话的主要内容、我所得出的有关喇嘛的结论以及他本人的主张都转告了英国驻华公使朱尔典和

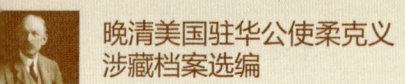
俄国大使廓索维慈。我认为，他们都很赞同我的意见。

This curious episode, this glimpse into pure Asiatic politics, seems to me a peculiar interest. I hope you will think likewise and pardon the length of my narrative.

这段有趣的插曲让我能窥见亚洲政治事务的冰山一角。我很感兴趣。我希望您也感兴趣，原谅我喋喋不休地讲了这么长。

Always faithfully yours

Rockhill

您忠诚的

柔克义

（二）中文剪报

柔克义以剪报的形式搜集了当时中文报纸有关 1908 年达赖喇嘛访问北京的新闻报道，并将其翻译成英文发回美国国务院。这些报纸主要有《中央日报》《顺天时报》等。

达赖喇嘛最近踪迹（大清光绪三十四年十月初七日）

初五日下午一钟，达赖喇嘛同堪布喇嘛等十二名，由雍和宫栋克尔喇嘛带路至玛嘎拉庙、松祝寺、北长街福佑寺、白塔寺各处佛殿，挂哈达行礼。至五点一刻始毕，又到庆王府、醇王府各馈哈达，至六钟二刻回雍和宫。沿途有外城总厅派巡警官兵保护。

Latest movements of the Dalai Lama

On the afternoon of the 5th. inst. (Oct, 29) at one o'clock the Dalai Lama, accompanied by the abbots and other lamas, (ten persons in all), was conducted by the Tongkhor of the Yung Ho Kung to visit the Ma-chia-la Temple, the Sung Chu Monastery, the Fu-yu Monastery on North Long Street, the White Pagoda and various other Buddhist shrines, where they presented scarfs and worshipped. The visits were not over until 5:15 p.m. After this they called at the palaces of the Prince Ch'ing and Prince Ch'un, where they also made presents of scarfs. At half past Six they returned to Yung Ho Kung. An escort of officers and patrolmen was furnished by the superintendent of Police of the Outer City.

(Oct. 30)

```
Group 10.    Tibetan Affairs.

Document 10 A.    Latest Movements of the Dalai Lama.

        On the afternoon of the 5th. inst. (Oct. 29) at one o'clock the Dalai Lama,
accompanied by the Abbots and other lamas, (ten persons in all), was conducted by
the Tongkhor of the Yung Ho Kung to visit the Ma-chia-la Temple, the Sung-chu
Monastery, the Fu-yu Monastery on North Long Street, the White Pagoda and various
other Buddhist shrines, where they presented scarfs and worshipped. The visits were
not over until 5:15 p.m. After this they called at the palaces of Prince Ch'ing and
Prince Ch'un, where they also made presents of scarfs. At half past six they re-
turned to the Yung Ho Kung. An escort of officers and patrolmen was furnished by the
Superintendent of Police of the Outer City.
                                (Oct. 30)
```

紫光阁赐宴补志

今日达赖在紫光阁筵宴已明见谕旨。闻所有应奏满蒙乐曲已经内务府传知乐部，敬谨预备云。

Banquet to the Dalai Lama at the Palace of Purple Light

To-day the Dalai Lama attended a banquet in the Palace of Purple Light, an edict concerning which has already been published. We learn that the Department of the Imperial Household notified the Board of Music, which secured musicians to sing Manchu and Mongol songs.

(No date)

Document 10 B.   Banquet to the Dalai Lama at the Palace of Purple Light.

To-day the Dalai Lama attended a banquet in the Place of Purple Light, an edict concerning which has already been published. We learn that the Department of the Imperial Household notified the Board of Music, which secured musicians to sing Manchu and Mongol songs.

(No date)

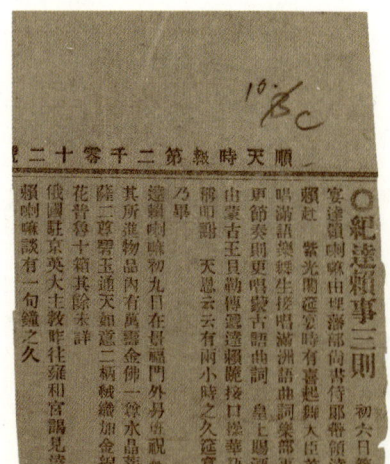

纪达赖事三则（《顺天时报》第 2020 号）

初六日筵宴，达赖喇嘛由理藩部尚书侍郎带领。达赖赴紫光阁筵宴时有喜起舞，大臣首唱满语乐，舞生接唱满洲语曲词，乐部再更节奏，则更唱蒙古语曲词。皇上赐酒，由蒙古王贝勒传递达赖跪接，口操华语称叩谢天恩云云。有两小时之久筵宴乃毕。

达赖喇嘛初九日在景福门外另班祝。其所进物品中有万寿金佛一尊、水晶菩萨二尊、碧玉通天如意二柄、绒织加金线花普鲁十箱，其余未详。

俄国驻京英大主教昨往雍和宫谒见达赖喇嘛，谈有一旬钟之久。

Three Items Concerning the Dalai Lama

On the 6th inst. (Oct 30), the officers of the Ministry of Dependencies entertained the Dalai Lama at a feast in the Palace of Purple Light. There was a theatrical performance and an exhibition of dancing during the banquet. The manager of the company of the players sang in Manchu and musicians and dancers joined in the songs. The Board of Music then requested a change of programme, and they sang Mongol songs in Mongol speech. The Emperor sent a present of wine, which was conveyed by the Mongol Princes to the Dalai Lama, who knelt and expressed his thanks. After two hours the banquet ended.

On the 9th. inst. the Dalai Lama made a distribution of gifts outside the Ching Fu Gate. Among the presents given were a golden image of Buddha, two crystal images of Buddhisatvas, two green jade sceptres, and ten boxes of Pu-Lu velvet inwrought with gold thread. The other presents were not mentioned.

Bishop Ying, of the Russian Church in Peking, went yesterday to Yung Ho Kung to pay his respects to the Dalai Lama, and had a brief conversation with him.

（No Date）

Document 10 C. Three Items Concerning the Dalai Lama.

On the 6th. inst. (Oct 30) the officers of the Ministry of Dependencies entertained the Dalai Lama at a feast in the Palace of Purple Light. There was a theatrical performance and an exhibition of dancing during the banquet. The manager of the company of players sang in Manchu and the musicians and dancers joined in the songs. The Board of Music then requested a change of programme, and they sang Mongol songs in Mongol speech. The Emperor sent a present of wine, which was conveyed by the Mongol Princes to the Dalai Lama, who knelt and expressed his thanks. After two hours the banquet ended.

On the 9th. inst. the Dalai Lama made a distribution of gifts outside the Ching Fu Gate. Among the presents given were a golden image of the Buddha, two crystal images of Boddhisatvas, two green jade sceptres, and ten boxes of Pu-lu velvet inwrought with gold thread. The other presents were not mentioned.

Bishop Ying, of the Russian Church in Peking, went yesterday to the Yung Ho Kung to pay his respects to the Dalai Lama, and had a brief conversation with him.

(No date)

温大臣赴藏近闻（1908年）

新简驻藏大臣温宗尧日昨有折来京。内容略云藏务关系非常紧要，须迅速到任，拟请改由海道前赴藏任。兹闻请将吴采亮等员随往以资得力云。

Resident Wen Goes to Tibet

We learn that a communication came to Peking a few days ago from H.E. Wen Tsung-Yao, appointed the Imperial Resident for Tibet, saying that the conditions in Tibet were unusually serious and he ought to take his appointment at once. He proposed to ask permission to go by sea to Tibet (by India), and to take with him Wu Ts'ai-Liang and others as attaches to assist him.

(No date)

Group 10, Tibetan Affairs.   2

Document 10 D.   Resident Wen Goes to Tibet.

     We learn that a communication came to Peking a few days ago from H.E. Wen Tsung-Yao, appointed Imperial Resident for Tibet, saying that the conditions in Tibet were unusually serious and that he ought to take up his appointment at once. He proposed to ask permission to go by sea to Tibet (by India), and to take with him Wu Ts'ai-Liang and others as attaches to assist him.

            (No date)

张荫棠请西藏先设农垦植物研究所

外务部张丞堂荫棠与理藩部寿尚书条议，西藏人民农务皆守旧俗，种植垦牧各项事宜向不研究整顿。应先令驻藏办事大臣赵季帅选派精于西藏语言文字人员，在西藏要隘设立农垦植物研究所，每日宣讲改良农垦植物之办法，并贴藏文劝谕告示劝导藏民入所听讲以收实效。闻寿尚书颇为赞成，闻已与溥尚

116

Document 10 E.   An Agricultural Station Proposed for Tibet.

H.E. Chang Yin-T'ang, Counselor of the Foreign Office, has consulted with H.E. Shou, the Minister of Dependencies, concerning the antiquated methods of agriculture practiced in Tibet. He stated that in the matters of agriculture, horticulture and cattle breeding the Tibetans have never made any progress. He suggested that orders ought to be sent first of all to General Chao Chi, the Acting Imperial Resident of Tibet, to appoint an official familiar with Tibetan speech and writing, to establish in some appropriate valley of Tibet an experiment station for agriculture and horticulture, and that such an official should give daily instruction in improved methods of agriculture and horticulture, that he ought also to post a proclamation in Tibetan, urging the people of Tibet to visit the station and listen to the instruction so that they might put it into practice. We hear that the Minister of Dependencies is disposed to approve of the plan, and that he has already proposed to Minister P'u (probably Minister of Agriculture) certain regulations which if agreed upon will be put into force.

(No date)

书刻拟规章，俟拟妥即可施行云。

An Agricultural Station Proposed for Tibet

H.E. Chang Yin-T'ang, Counselor of the Foreign Office, has consulted with H.E. Shou, the Minister of Dependencies, concerning the antiquated method of agriculture practiced in Tibet. He stated that in the matters of agriculture, horticulture and cattle breeding the Tibetans have never made any progress. He suggested that orders ought to be sent first of all to General Chao Chi, the Acting Imperial Resident of Tibet, to appoint an official familiar with Tibetan speech and writing, to establish in some appropriate valley of Tibetan an experiment station for agriculture, and horticulture, and that such an official should give daily instructions in improved methods of agriculture and horticulture, that he ought also to post a proclamation in Tibetan, urging the people of Tibet to visit the station and listen to the instruction so that they may put it into practice. We hear that the Minister of Dependencies is disposed to approve of the plan, and that he has already proposed to the Minister P'u (probably Minister of Agriculture) certain regulations which if agreed upon will be put into force.

（No Date）

117

Document 10 F.   The Dalai to Witness Imperial Birthday Ceremonies.

On the occasion of the celebration of the birthday of Her Imperial Majesty the Empress Dowager the ceremonies in the palace and the festivities in the capital will be very interesting. The Dalai Lama is eager to go about and witness everything, so as to enlarge his experience. He has already so notified the Ministry of Dependencies, which has transmitted the request to the Home Office and to the Yamen of the Gendarmerie in the hope that they will make due preparations (for his protection).

(No date)

达赖欲遍览万寿礼仪

达赖喇嘛以皇太后万寿圣节在迩，都中庆贺万寿圣典礼仪极形热闹。达赖拟遍为游览以广智识，已通知理藩部转咨民政部步军统领衙门以期预备云。

The Dalai to Witness the Imperial Birthday Ceremonies

On the occasion of the celebration of the birthday of Her Imperial Majesty the Empress Dowager the ceremonies in the palace and festivities in the capital will be very interesting. The Dalai Lama is eager to go about and witness everything, so as to enlarge his experience. He has already notified the Ministry of Dependencies, which has transmitted to request to the Home Office and to the Yamen of the Gerdarmerie in the hope that they will make due preparations.

（No Date）

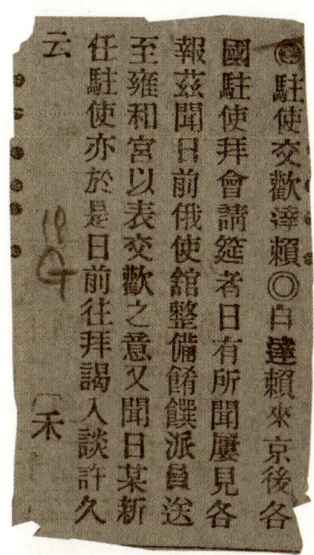

驻使交欢达赖

自达赖来京后各国驻使拜会请筵者日有所闻，屡见各报。兹闻日前俄使馆整备看馔派员送至雍和宫以表交欢之意。又闻日某新任驻使亦于是日前往拜谒，入谈许久云。

The Dalai Lama and the Foreign Representatives in Peking

Since the coming of the Dalai Lama to Peking the various representatives here of the foreign governments have called upon him to pay their respects and have entertained him, as has frequently been reported in the press. We now learn that a few days ago the Russian Legation prepared a lot of table delicacies which they sent to Yung Ho Kung by the hand of an officer as an evidence of friendship. We learn, too, that on the same day a certain newly arrived Minister of one of the Powers called to pay his respects, and had quite a long conversation with His Holiness.

(No date)

Document 10 G.　The Dalai Lama and the Foreign Representatives in Peking.

Since the coming of the Dalai Lama to Peking the various representatives here of the foreign governments have called upon him to pay their respects and have entertained him, as has frequently been reported in the press. We now learn that a few days ago the Russian Legation prepared a lot of table delicacies which they sent to the Yung Ho Kung by the hand of an officer as an evidence of friendship. We learn, too, that on the same day a certain newly arrived Minister of one of the Powers called to pay his respects, and had quite a long conversation with His Holiness.

(No date)

达赖回避中外官谒见日期

达赖喇嘛谕传堪布饬知门役，由初二三四五等日，如有东西各国宦商及中政府，除奉旨有特要事件外，其中外官府来寺者，概行回避免见云云。（上述避见日期为 1908 年 10 月 26 日至 29 日）

Days on which the Dalai Lama Can Not Receive Chinese and Foreign Officials

The Dalai Lama has directed the Four Abbots to instruct the Gate Guards that on the 2nd, 3rd, 4th and 5th of the month His Holiness will be unable to receive any Chinese or Foreign Officials who call at the temple, except those who came by Imperial Command on important business.

(These dates were included between Oct. 26 and 29, 1908)

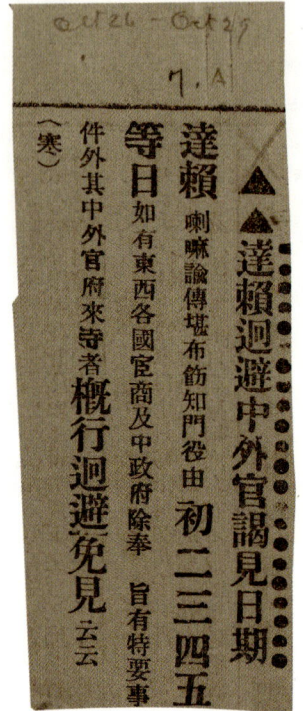

Rockhill Papers,

Translations from the Chinese.

Group 7, Tibetan Affairs, October 29 and 30. (1908).

Document 7 A. Days on which the Dalai Lama can not receive Chinese and Foreign Officials.
    The Dalai Lama has directed the Four Abbots to instruct the Gate Guards that on the 2d. 3d. 4th. and 5th of the month His Holiness will be unable to receive any Chinese or foreign officials who call at the Temple, except those who come by Imperial Command on important business.
            (These dates were included between Oct.26 and 29,1908)

纪达赖事二则

达赖喇嘛此次来京，凡京师风俗人情拟一一详细调查。闻现已向寿尚书商议领阅看善扑营，贯交该营。已传各等布阔人员日前在紫光阁演习以预备达预阅看云。

闻达赖喇嘛日前恭进御用马二匹。闻均一律黄色，标壮雄伟，性颇驯良。现已由上驷院饲养矣。

Two Items Related to the Dalai Lama

1.The Dalai Lama on coming to Peking has decided to make a detailed study of the customs and the social conditions here. We learn that he has already consulted with His Excellency, Minister Shou, and arranged an exhibition of wrestling. Those concerned with this a few days ago published the matter abroad and a number of men gathered at the Tzu Kuang Ko (Pavilion of Purple Light) to practice preparatory to giving an exhibition for the Dalai Lama.

2.We learned that the Dalai Lama a few days ago presented to the Imperial Court two beautiful sorrel horses. They have all the appearance of being fine strong animals, teachable and gentle. They have already been sent to the Imperial Stables.

(No Date)

Document 7 B. Two Items relating to the Dalai Lama.

1

The Dalai Lama on coming to Peking has decided to make a detailed study of the customs and social conditions here. We learn that he has already consulted with His Excellency, Minister Shou, and arranged for an exhibition of wrestling. Those concerned with this a few days ago published the matter abroad and a number of men gathered at the Tzu Kuang Ko (Pavilion of Purple Light) to practice preparatory to giving an exhibition for the Dalai Lama.

2 presented to the Imperial Court two
We learn that the Dalai Lama a few days ago beautiful sorrel horses. They have all the appearance of being fine strong animals, teacable and gentle. They have already been sent to the Imperial Stables.

(No date)

达赖移驻雍和宫近闻（光绪三十四年十月初五日）

达赖拟移驻雍和宫一节理藩部不日入奏，并于初一日先奏明达赖将暂住雍和宫，讲经三日，当蒙允准于初二日下午一时赴雍和宫，有警队护送。闻已于初四日仍回黄寺住锡云。

The Dalai Lama at the Yung Ho Kung

We learn that concerning the proposal of the Dalai Lama to move to the Yung Ho Kung (Lama Temple in Peking) the Ministry of Dependencies has just memorialized, moreover that a memorial was first sent in on 1st inst. (Oct. 25) stating clearly that the Dalai Lama wanted to stay temporarily at the Yung Ho Kung, mentioning a period of three days. At that time permission was granted and on the 2nd. inst. at one o'clock p.m. he went to the said lamasery escorted by a guard of policemen. We hear also that on the 4th. inst. he returned to the Yellow Temple to stay.

(October 29, 1908)

Document 7 C.   The Dalai Lama at the Yung Ho Kung.

We learn that concerning the proposal of the Dalai Lama to move to the Yung Ho Kung (Lama Temple in Peking) the Ministry of Dependencies has just memorialized, moreover that a memorial was first sent in on the 1st inst.(Oct.25) stating clearly that the Dalai Lama wanted to stay temporarily at the Yung Ho Kung, mentioning a period of three days. At that time permission was granted and on the 2d. inst. at one o'clock p.m. he went to the said lamasery escorted by a guard of policemen. We hear also that on the 4th. inst. he returned to the Yellow Temple to stay.

(October 29,1908)

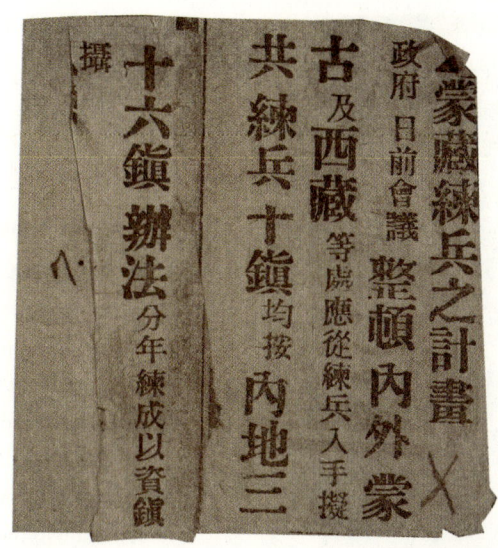

蒙藏练兵之计划

政府日前会议整顿内外蒙古及西藏等处应从练兵入手。拟共练兵十镇，均按内地三十六镇办法，分年练成，以资镇摄。

Strength of Forces for Mongolia and Tibet

A few days ago the Government consulted about the reorganization of the military forces for Inner and Outer Mongolia and Tibet. This will require the enlistment and drilling of new recruits. It is proposed to organize altogether ten brigades, which are to be modeled on the pattern of the provincial forces. After the drilling is completed they will serve in regular rotation in different places.

(No date)

Document 7 X.   Strength of Forces for Mongolia and Tibet.

　　A few days ago the Government consulted about the reorganization of the military forces for Inner and Outer Mongolia and Tibet. This will require the enlistment and drilling of new recruits. It is proposed to organize altogether ten brigades, which are to be modelled on the pattern of the provincial forces. After the drilling is completed they will serve in regular rotation in different places.
(No date)

达赖住雍和宫三天

达赖喇嘛现虽移居雍和宫，并非久住，已由理藩部奏准达赖在雍和宫唪经三日后仍回黄寺云。

The Dalai Lama's Three Days' Visit to the Yung Ho Kung

Although the Dalai Lama has gone to the Yung Ho Kung, he is not to stay there long. The Ministry of Dependencies memorialized the Throne and obtained a Rescript, saying:

"The Dalai Lama may conduct services for three days at the Yung Ho Kung, after which he will return again to the Yellow Temple."

(No date)

Group 7, Tibetan Affairs.   2

Document 7 D.   The Dalai Lama's Three Days' Visit to the Yung Ho Kung.

Although the Dalai Lama has gone to the Yung Ho Kung, he is not to stay there long.   The Ministry of Dependencies memorialized the Throne and obtained a Rescript, saying:-
"The Dalai Lama may conduct services for three days at the Yung Ho Kung, after which he will return again to the Yellow Temple."
(No date)

达赖对于藏政之意见

（1908年10月29日）

近日枢府与达赖会议藏政
一节，屡志前报，兹探得
确实消息，其议定之办法
共有四端：（一）速改官
制；（二）慎重交涉；（三）
提倡实业；（四）缓设行省。
并闻万寿，前即由理藩部
具折代奏云。

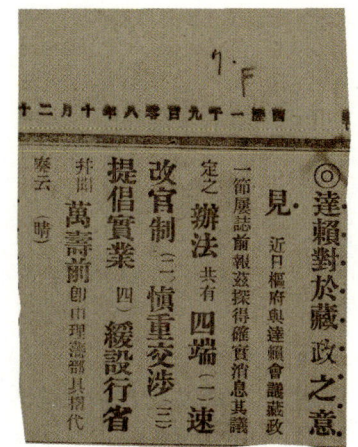

The Dalai Lama's Views as to the Government of Tibet

During several days past the Cabinet has discussed with the Dalai Lama the question of the government of Peking. The matter has been noted in several previous issues of this journal. A further enquiry now for the facts discloses that four things have been agreed upon.

(1) The administration is to be reorganized, (2) There must be great caution exercised to prevent foreign entanglements, (3) Industrial development is to be promoted, and (4) the setting up of provincial governments is to be postponed.

(October 29, 1908)

Document 7 F. The Dalai Lama's Views as to the Government of Tibet.

During several days past the Cabinet has discussed with the Dalai Lama the question of the government of Peking. The matter has been noted in several previous issues of this journal. A further enquiry now for the facts discloses that four things have been agreed upon.

(1) The administration is to be reorganized, (2) There must be great caution exercised to prevent foreign entanglements, (3) Industrial development is to be promoted, and (4) the setting up of provincial governments is to be postponed.

We hear also that the Ministry of Dependencies will prepare and submit a memorial in the above sense before the Imperial Birthday.

(October 29)

达赖与英公使（《中央日报》）

闻达赖喇嘛自来京后与英国驻京公
使情谊颇笃，近日屡次互相谒拜。
昨九月二十九日系达赖敬佛之期，
英公使遣随员恭备番菜果品等项，
送往黄寺。闻达赖一律收下云。

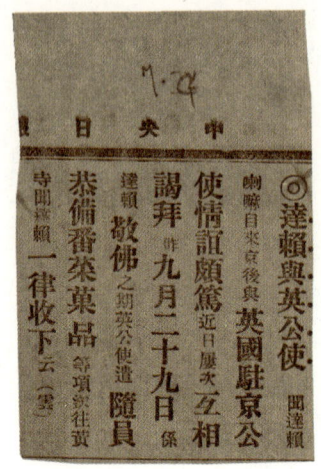

Relations of the Dalai Lama with the British Minister

Since the arrival of the Dalai Lama
in Peking his relations with the British
Minister have tended to become rather
friendly. Recently a number of times they
have exchanged calls, and yesterday, on
the 29th, of the Ninth Moon (Oct 23),
on which the Dalai Lama was observing
a Buddhist festival, the British Minister
had his staff prepare a present of Tibetan
delicacies and fruits which he sent to the
Yellow Temple. We learn that the present
was accepted by the Dalai Lama.

(No date)

Document 7 G.   Relations of the Dalai Lama with the British Minister.

Since the arrival of the Dalai Lama in Peking his relations with the British
Minister have tended to become rather friendly. Recently a number of times they have
exchanged calls, and yesterday, on the 29th. of the Ninth Moon (Oct. 23), on which
the Dalai Lama was observing a Buddhist festival, the British Minister had his staff
prepare a present of Tibetan delicacies and fruits which he sent to the Yellow Temple
We learn that the present was accepted by the Dalai Lama.
(No date)

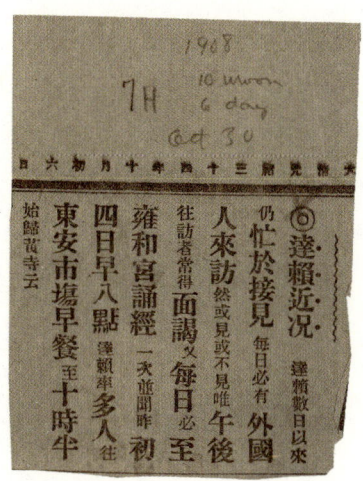

达赖近况

达赖数日以来仍忙于接见，每日必有外国人来访，然或见或不见。唯午后往访者常得面谒，又每日必至雍和宫诵经一次。并闻昨初四日早八点，达赖率多人往东安市场早餐，至十时半始归黄寺云。

The Dalai Lama Very Busy

During the past few days the Dalai Lama has been overburdened with callers. Every day numbers of foreigners come to make enquiries. No matter whether his response is or is not that he will receive them, daily those who go to make enquiries always have a personal interview. Moreover he must go every day to the Yung Ho Kung to read one service. We hear also that on the 4th. instant he went at eight o'clock in the morning to the Tung An Shih Ch'ang to breakfast, and did not return to the Yellow Temple until half past ten in the morning.

(Oct. 30)

Document 7 H.   The Dalai Lama Very Busy.

During the past few days the Dalai Lama has been overburdened with callers. Every day numbers of foreigners come to make enquiries. No matter whether his response is or is not that he will receive them, daily those who go to make enquiries always have a personal interview. Moreover he must go every day to the Yung Ho Kung to read one service. We hear also that on the 4th. instant he went at eight o'clock in the morning to the Tung An Shih Ch'ang to breakfast, and did not return to the Yellow Temple until half past ten in the morning.

(Oct. 30)

达赖对于世界大势之感慨

达赖学习汉文一节已志前报。兹闻所聘之汉文教授某君为保阳学校之毕业生，国文极精深，藏语又颇娴熟，并于世界大势亦能知其梗概。每日将日人对于朝鲜之政策择其最足动人者译以藏语，达赖闻之遂仰天叹曰：今而后吾知同教之不足持也。言毕泪下。

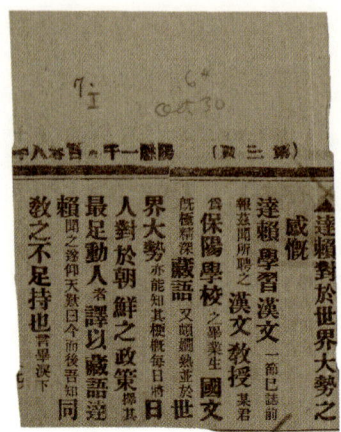

The Dalai Lama Moved by World Conditions

In a previous issue we reported that the Dalai Lama had taken up the study of Chinese. We now learn that he has engaged as teacher of Chinese a gentleman who is a graduate of the Pao Yang School. He is thoroughly versed in our national literature and he has some acquaintance with Tibetan. He is also able to inform the Dalai Lama as to world affairs generally. One day he selected the essential facts as to Japanese policy in Korea, which he translated into Tibetan. The Dalai, after listening to him, lifted his eyes to Heaven and sighed, saying: "Henceforth I know that our religion is insufficient for our protection". As he spoke the tears fell from his eyes.

(Oct. 30)

Document 7 I.   The Dalai Lama Moved by World Conditions.

In a previous issue we reported that the Dalai Lama had taken up the study of Chinese. We now learn that he has engaged as teacher of Chinese a gentleman who is a graduate of the Pao Yang School. He is thoroughly versed in our national literature and he has some acquaintance with Tibetan. He is also able to inform the Dalai Lama as to world affairs generally. One day he selected the essential facts as to Japanese policy in Korea, which he translated into Tibetan. The Dalai, after listening to him, lifted his eyes to Heaven and sighed, saying: "Henceforth I know that our religion is insufficient for our protection". As he spoke the tears fell from his eyes.

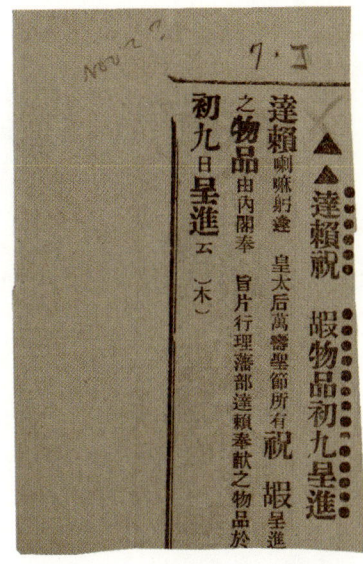

达赖祝嘏物品初九呈进

达赖喇嘛躬逢皇太后万寿圣节，所有祝嘏呈进之物品由内阁奉旨片行理藩部，达赖奉献之物品于初九日呈进云。

A Birthday Present from the Dalai Lama

On the 9th. instant the Dalai Lama sent a number of birthday presents to the Empress Dowager. The Grand Secretariat has now received an Edict making acknowledgement of the same.

(Nov. 2.?)

```
Group 7, Tibetan Affairs.                    5


Document 7 J.  A Birthday Present from the Dalai Lama.

        On the 9th. instant the Dalai Lama sent a number of birthday presents to the
Empress Dowager. The Grand Secretariat has now received an Edict making acknowledge-
ment, of the same.

                    (Nov. 2. ?)
```

Document 7 K.   The Dalai Lama Presents Buddhist Images.

On the 10th. of the Tenth Moon (Nov. 3), the birthday of Her Imperial Majest
the Empress Dowager, the Dalai Lama, so we hear, sent her a present of three Buddhist images. One was decorated with kingfisher feathers, one set with diamonds,
and the third with pearls. Together they were worth several hundred thousand taels.

达赖祝嘏佛像三尊

十月初十万寿节闻达赖预备祝嘏贡品计佛像三尊，一系翠质，一系金刚钻石质，一系珍珠质，价值约在数十万云。

The Dalai Lama Presents Buddhist Images

On the 10th, of the Tenth Moon (Nov.3), the birthday of Her Imperial Majesty the Empress Dowager, the Dalai Lama, so we hear, sent her a present of three Buddhist Images. One was decorated with kingfisher feathers, one set with diamonds, and the third with pearls. Together they were worth several hundred thousand taels.

达赖与俄主教谈传教事

俄国北堂若诺肯提大主教日前拜谒达赖喇嘛，互以俄语问答约计两小时之久。闻通晓俄语人云，达赖与主教所谈者多系有关传教之事。

The Dalai Lama Talks with the Russian Archbishop of Missionary Work

The Very Reverend Jo-No-K'en-Ti, the Archbishop of the Russian Church in Peking, called a few days ago upon the Dalai Lama to pay his respects. They conversed together for about two hours in the Russian language. We learn from one who understands Russian that the subject of their conversation for the most part related to missionary work.

(No date)

Document 7 M.　The Dalai Lama Talks with the Russian Archbishop of Missionary Work.

The Very Reverend Jo-No-K'en-Ti, the Archbishop of the Russian Church in Peking, called a few days ago upon the Dalai Lama to pay his respects. They conversed together for about two hours in the Russian language. We learn from one who understands Russian that the subject of their conversation for the most part related to missionary work.

(No date)

131

御赐达赖对联文

皇帝御赐达赖对联，原文系某相国所撰。其
文曰：大千世界参真谛，亿万斯年拱上京。

The Dalai Lama Receives a Pair of Scrolls

His Imperial Majesty the Emperor has presented to the Dalai Lama a pair of autographed scrolls. The sentiment was composed in a certain dependency[1] and is as follows:

"Through thousands of worlds* he has taught the truth."

"After millions of years *he has come to Peking."

(No date)

Document 7 N.   The Dalai Lama Receives a Pair of Scrolls.

His Imperial Majesty the Emperor has presented to the Dalai Lama a pair of autographed scrolls. The sentiment was composed in a certain dependency and is as follows:-

"Through thousands of worlds*he has taught the truth."
"After millions of years*he has come to Peking."
(No date)

---

[1] 这里柔克义误解了"相国"的含义，故翻译成 "Dependency"——编者

开议藏务志闻

顷得确实消息，政府诸公现已决定，万寿节后与达赖开议西藏各项要政，因驻藏大臣屡次电告藏地紧要情形，催促达赖回藏。达赖亦不欲在京度岁，故一俟各项要政议妥即行陛辞出京云。

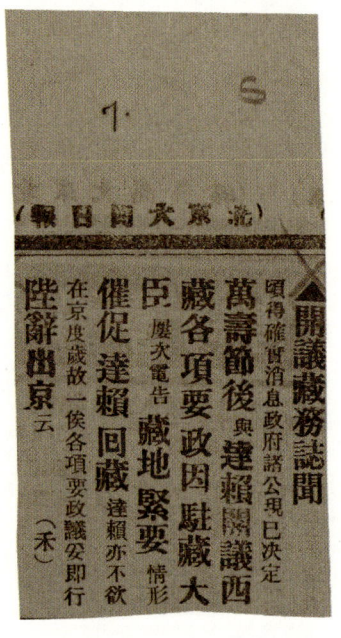

Tibetan Affairs to be Discussed

We have just learned that it is true that the officers of the Government have decided to take up the discussion of all important questions relating to Tibet as soon as the festivities attending the Imperial birthday are concluded. This is because the Imperial Resident has repeatedly telegraphed reporting the serious condition of affairs there and urging the return of the Dalai Lama to his capital. The Dalai Lama, moreover, does not want to pass the New Years in Peking, and as soon as important matters are satisfactorily settled he will leave the Capital and begin his homeward journey.

(No date)

Document 7 S.　Tibetan Affairs to be Discussed.

We have just learned that it is true that the officers of the Government have decided to take up the discussion of all important questions relating to Tibet as soon as the festivities attending the Imperial birthday are concluded. This is because the Imperial Resident has repeatedly telegraphed reporting the serious condition of affairs there and urging the return of the Dalai Lama to his capital. The Dalai Lama, moreover, does not want to pass the New Years in Peking, and as soon as important matters are satisfactorily settled he will leave the Capital and begin his homeward journey.

(No date)

拟画清西藏政教界限

各军机连日就达赖处会商划清宗教政治界限，免达赖与驻藏大臣争执。

The Limits of Ecclesiastical Authority in Tibet

Recently for several days in succession the Ministers of the Grand Council held conferences with the Dalai Lama, with a view to defining the limits of the authority of the Lama Government in Tibet, so as to avoid possible friction between the Dalai Lama and the Imperial Resident.

(No date)

Document 7 T. The Limits of Ecclesiastical Authority in Tibet.

Recently for several days in succession the Ministers of the Grand Council held conferences with the Dalai Lama, with a view to defining the limits of the authority of the Lama Government in Tibet, so as to avoid possible friction between the Dalai Lama and the Imperial Resident.
(No date)

134

西藏问题

日前政府会议西藏事宜，有派理藩部寿子年尚书、张荫棠丞堂前往西藏先行调查，再逐渐办理之意。所有训练精兵一节，已责成泽公由部筹款并详订办法。

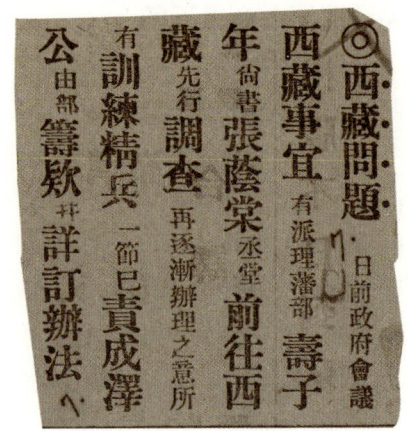

The Tibetan Question

A few days ago the Government considered Tibetan affairs and appointed H. E. Chou Tzu-Nien Minister of Dependencies, and Chang Yin-T'ang the Vice Ministers as Commissioners to proceed to Tibet, to make a preliminary investigation of the situation there with a view to introducing gradually the needed reforms. With respect to the training and drilling of the picked troops Duke Tae was charged with this duty, and the Minister was directed to appropriate the necessary funds as well as to draw up the detailed regulations.

(No date)

Group 7, Tibetan Affairs.   8

Document 7 U.   The Tibetan Question.

A few days ago the Government considered Tibetan affairs and appointed H.E. Chou Tzu-Nien Minister of Dependencies, and Chang Yin-T'ang the Vice Ministers as Commissioners to proceed to Tibet, to make a preliminary investigation of the situation there with a view to introducing gradually the needed reforms. With respect to the training and drilling of the picked troops Duke Tae was charged with this duty, and the Ministry was directed to appropriate the necessary funds as well as to draw up the detailed regulations.

(No date)

藏政改期会商之近闻

会议政务王大臣前拟初二日会订西藏政事，实行整顿次序各节，今已改为万寿后十二日，会拟办法探之。系因达赖喇嘛所拟整顿西藏之详细要点节略已于日前呈递理藩部，并闻该部寿尚书因将届万寿未克代奏，一俟译成汉文再行奏陈备案并议，故现改为十二日议办云。

Change of Date for Conference on Tibet

We now learn that the Princes and Ministers of the Council of State, who had arranged to meet on the 2nd inst. (Oct. 26) to considered matters connected with the Tibetan Government and to introduce gradually certain reforms have postponed the meeting until after the Imperial birthday. They are now to meet on the 12th inst. (Nov. 5) to determine the procedure. On enquiry we discovered that the change was due to the fact that a plan for the reorganization of the dependency which the Dalai Lama had prepared was submitted a few days ago to the Ministry of Dependencies, and that on account of the approaching celebration of the Imperial birthday the Minister was unable to prepare a memorial to send in with it. As soon as it is translated into Chinese it will be presented. The date of the meeting, therefore, has been changed to the 12th. when the matter will be duly considered.

(No date)

Document 7 V.   Change of Date for Conference on Tibet.
of the Council of State
We now learn that the Princes and Ministers, who had arranged to meet on the 2nd. inst. (Oct. 26) to considered matters connected with the Tibetan Government and to introduce gradually certain reforms have postponed the meeting until after the Imperial birthday. They are now to meet on the 12th. inst. (Nov. 5) to determine the proceedure. On enquiry we discovered that the change was due to the fact that a plan for the reorganization of the dependency which the Dalai Lama had prepared was submitted a few days ago to the Ministry of Dependencies, and that on account of the approaching celebration of the Imperial birthday the Minister was unable to prepare a memorial to send in with it. As soon as it is translated into Chinese it will be presented. The date of the meeting, therefore, has been changed to the 12th. when the matter will be duly considered.
(No date)

预备藏改行省

西藏改建行省事政府已拟从缓办理。昨得政界消息云，近日军机处各亲王大臣业已详查《西藏全图》，按照图中界限划分清楚，参定应于何处建设省会，于何处建制官缺，以为将来改建行省之预备。

The Provincial Organization of Tibet

The proposed organization of Tibet into provinces was postponed by the Government, but yesterday we learned from official circles that on that day the Imperial Princes and Ministers of the Cabinet had given very careful study to the map of Tibet, with a view to clearly demarking the boundaries of the proposed provinces. They also consulted as to the best places for establishing the provincial assemblies and stationing the various officers, in preparation for the setting up in the future of provincial governments.

(No date)

Document 7 W.   The Provincial Organization of Tibet.

The proposed organization of Tibet into provinces was postponed by the Government, but yesterday we learned from official circles that on that day the Imperial Princes and Ministers of the Cabinet had given very careful study to the map of Tibet, with a view to clearly demarking the boundaries of the proposed provinces. They also consulted as to the best places for establishing the provincial assemblies and stationing the various officers, in preparation for the setting up in the future of provincial governments.

(No date)

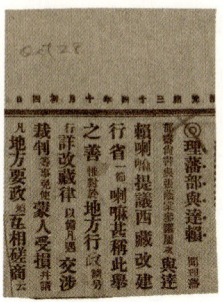

理藩部与达赖（《中央日报》1908 年 10 月 28 日）

闻理藩部寿尚书与张荫棠参议屡次与达赖喇嘛提议西藏改建行省一节。喇嘛甚称此举之善，惟对于地方行政，请另行详改藏律，以备凡遇交涉裁判等事，免使蒙人受损，并请凡地方要政须互相磋商云。

The Minister of Dependencies confers with the Dalai Lama

We learn that His Excellency, Shou Shan, the Minister of Dependencies and His Excellency, Chang Yin-t'ang, have consulted a number of times with Dalai Lama concerning the proposal to divide Tibet into provinces. The Dalai Lama said emphatically that such a change would not harmonize with the administration of Tibet[1] and requested that certain changes be made in the laws relating to Tibet which would provide for any emergencies arising in foreign relations and thus any injury to the people would be avoided. He suggested, too, that any important matters of local concern could be managed by cooperation (of the Imperial and Tibetan authorities).

Document 9 C(1) The Minister of Dependencies confers with the Dalai Lama.

We learn that His Excellency, Shou Shan, the Minister of Dependencies and His Excellency, Chang Yin-t'ang, have consulted a number of times with the Dalai Lama concerning the proposal to divide Tibet into provinces. The Dalai Lama said emphatically that such a change would not harmonize with the administration of Tibet and requested that certain changes be made in the laws relating to Tibet which would provide for any emergencies arising in foreign relations and thus any injury to the people would be avoided. He suggested, too, that any important matters of local concern could be managed by cooperation of the Imperial and Tibetan authorities).

---

[1] 此处"此举之善"，柔克义翻译得不准确。

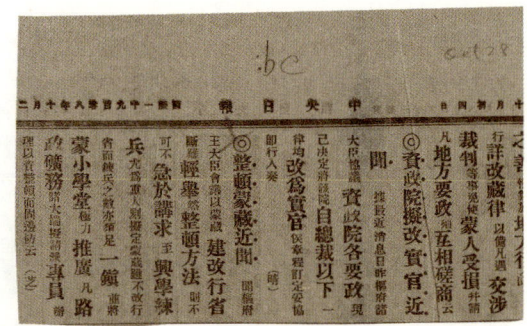

整顿蒙藏近闻（《中央日报》1908年10月28日）

闻枢府王大臣会议以蒙藏建改行省，断难轻举。然整顿方法，则不可不急于讲求，至兴学练兵，尤为重大。刻拟定蒙藏虽不改行省而练兵之数亦须足一镇，并将蒙小学堂极力推广。凡路政矿务诸大端，拟请派专员办理以资整顿而固边防云。

Recent Reports anent Reorganization of Mongolia and Tibet

We hear that the Princes and Ministers of the central Government have consulted together respecting the difficulties attending the organization of provinces in Mongolia and Tibet, which was so lightly proposed. The matter of introducing reforms is one that can not be too hastily pressed. Investigation is now being made concerning the establishment of schools and the training of soldiers as being more important, so it has been decided that, although Mongolia and Tibet are not to be divided into provinces, at least one brigade of troops should be organized and trained and the primary system of schools in Mongolia be extended. As to railway and mining matters it is proposed to memorialize and ask that specialists be put in charge of them so as to promote reform and strengthen the frontier defences.

(October 28)

Document 9 C (2)   Recent Reports anent Reorganization of Mongolia and Tibet.

We hear that the Princes and Ministers of the central Government have consulted together respecting the difficulties attending the organization of provinces in Mongolia and Tibet, which was so lightly proposed.   The matter of introducing reforms is one that can not be too hastily pressed.   Investigation is now being made concerning the establishment of schools and the training of soldiers as being more important, so it has been decided that, although Mongolia and Tibet are not to be divided into provinces, at least one brigade of troops should be organized and trained and the primary system of schools in Mongolia be extended.   As to railway and mining matters it is proposed to memorialize and ask that specialists be put in charge of them so as to promote reform and strengthen the frontier defences.

(October 28)

纪达赖事三则

达赖喇嘛于日昨初二日未刻率其徒
众堪布等赴雍和宫内诵经三日毕，
于初五日由雍和宫仍回黄寺，经理
藩部寿尚书已传知民政部及步军统
领衙门委派警兵翼兵于沿途妥为照
料矣。

Affairs of the Dalai (3)

On the 2nd. inst. between one and
three o'clock p.m. the Dalai Lama, with
his attendants and the Abbots, will go to
the Yung Ho Kung to remain for three
days to conduct services there. On the
5th. they will return from the Yung Ho
Kung to the Yellow Temple. The Minister
of Dependencies, H.E. Shou Shan, has
already notified the Home Office and the
Commandant of the Gendarmerie that
they may detail police and troops to be
stationed along the route for protection.

(No date)

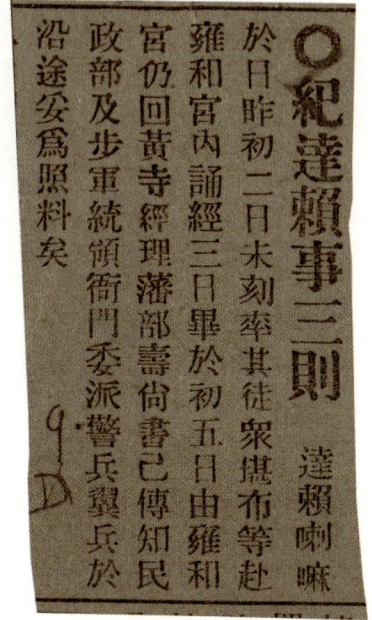

Group 9, Tibetan Affairs   3

Document 9 D.   Affairs of the Dalai (3).

On the 2nd. inst. between one and three o'clock p.m. the Dalai Lama, with
his attendants and the Abbots, will go to the Yung Ho Kung to remain for three days
to conduct services there. On the 5th. they will return from the Yung Ho Kung to
the Yellow Temple. The Minister of Dependencies, H.E. Shou Shan, has already notified the Home Office and the Commandant of the Gendarmerie that they may detail
police and troops to be stationed along the route for protection.
(No date)

前二日之达赖喇嘛

初二日为达赖受拜之期，有蒙古喇嘛二百余名谒见。又下午一点钟肃王、涛贝勒、理藩部尚书寿大人各送礼物多件。又四钟有路局总办治格赴黄寺一带查验道工，至五钟后进城。

News of the Dalai Lama

On the 2nd. inst. the Dalai Lama held a reception and more than two hundred Mongol lamas came to pay their respects. At one p.m. there also came Prince Su, Prince T'ao and H. E. Shou, the Minister of Dependencies, each one of whom brought presents. At four o'clock p.m. the Director General of Roads, Chih-ko, went to the Yellow Temple to inspect the work done on the road. He remained until five p.m. after which he returned to the city.

(No date)

Document 9 E.   News of the Dalai Lama.

On the 2nd. inst. the Dalai Lama held a reception and more than two hundred Mongol lamas came to pay their respects. At one p.m. there also came Prince Su, Prince T'ao and H.E. Shou, the Minister of Dependencies, each one of whom brought presents. At four o'clock p.m. the Director General of Roads, Chih-ko, went to the Yellow Temple to inspect the work done on the road. He remained until five p.m. after which he returned to the city.

(No date)

温大臣密陈藏政要折之传闻

新简驻藏办事大臣温宗尧日前随同谢
恩折另有密折一件，闻系条陈西藏应
兴应革诸要政，约有数千言，已蒙留
中披览。内容未详。

Minister Wen's Report on Tibet

H.E. Wen Tsung-Yao, the Imperial
Resident of Tibet, a few days since followed up
his memorial of thanks with a secret report. We
hear that it contains in a number of articles a
list of the measures proposed for Tibet, noting
those that ought to be adopted and those that
should be amended. There are several thousand
words in the memorial. The Rescript directs
that it is to be retained for examination. The
contents are not known in detail.

(No date)

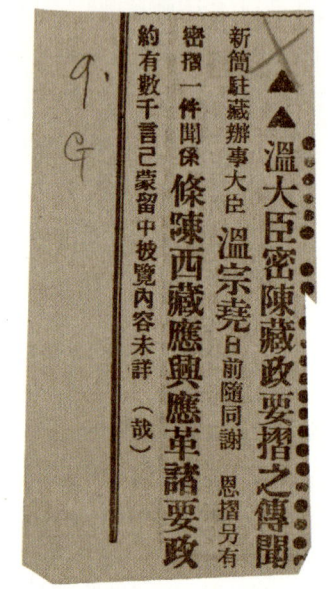

Document 9 G.   Minister Wen's Report on Tibet.

        H.E. Wen Tsung-Yao, the Imperial Resident of Tibet, a few days since fol-
lowed up his memorial of thanks with a secret report. We hear that it contains in
a number of articles a list of the measures proposed for Tibet, noting those that
ought to be adopted and those that should be amended. There are several thousand
words in the memorial. The Rescript directs that it is to be retained for examination. The contents are not known in detail.
                            (No date)

达赖参观学堂之筹备

达赖参观京师各学堂已志本报。昨学部接理藩部文称，请派员导引该部荣尚书，以达赖观学之举关系甚大，最宜郑重，拟于日内先行通知各学堂，定日派员会同理藩部引导达赖，先由京师大学堂次第参观，再行照会民政、陆军两部，分别参观陆军、警察各学堂云。

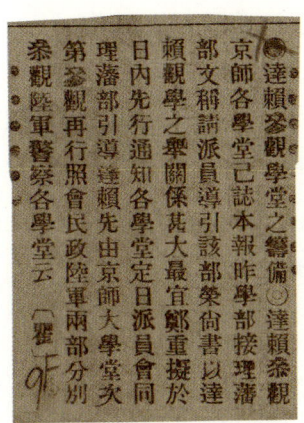

Preparation for the Dalai's Visit to the Schools

That the Dalai is to inspect the Peking schools has already been noted in our journal. Yesterday the Board of Education received a note from the Minister of Dependencies requesting that an officer of that Board be detailed to conduct His Holiness. The Minister of Education replied that the proposed visit of the Dalai Lama would be most appropriate, and, being a matter of importance, he intended within a few days to notify the schools in advance, fixing a time for the inspection. He would also send an officer to accompany the representative of the Ministry of Dependencies and escort the Dalai Lama. They would first visit the University and then make an inspection of the other grades in succession. Notices were also sent to the Home Office and the War Office, with requests for details of police and soldiers to be stationed at each school for protection[1].

(No date)

Document 9 F.   Preparation for the Dalai's Visit to the Schools.

That the Dalai is to inspect the Peking schools has already been noted in our journal. Yesterday the Board of Education received a note from the Minister of Dependencies requesting that an officer of that Board be detailed to conduct His Holiness. The Minister of Education replied that the proposed visit of the Dalai Lama would be most appropriate, and, being a matter of importance, he intended within a few days to notify the schools in advance, fixing a time for the inspection. He would also send an officer to accompany the representative of the Ministry of Dependencies and escort the Dalai Lama. They would first visit the University and then make an inspection of the other grades in succession. Notices were also sent to the Home Office and the War Office, with requests for details of police and soldiers to be stationed at each school for protection.

(No date)

---

[1]　原文"分别参观陆军、警察各学堂"，柔克义理解翻译有误。

会议藏政已有端倪

西藏改建行省，凡一切开矿练兵各事，均经张大臣荫棠与达赖商议，现已渐就范围。外间传闻达赖硬阻各项新政，实系传闻之误云。

A Conference on the Government of Tibet

H. E. Chang Yin-T'ang and the Dalai Lama have been conferring together on the matter of organizing Tibet into provinces and those relating to mining and military affairs. They are now gradually approaching the end. There is a report in outside circles that the Dalai Lama is obstreperous and opposes all the proposed measures, considering reform to be a mistake[1].

(No date)

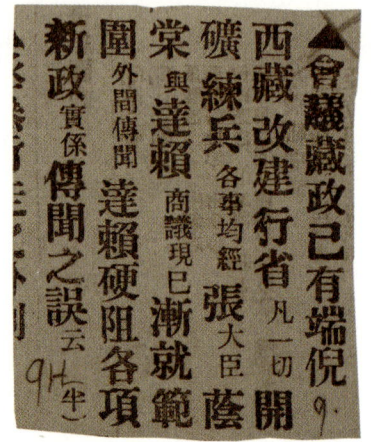

Group 9, Tibetan Affairs. 4

Document 9 H. A Conference on the Government of Tibet.

H.E. Chang Yin-T'ang and the Dalai Lama have been conferring together on the matter of organizing Tibet into provinces and those relating to mining and military affairs. They are now gradually approaching the end. There is a report in outside circles that the Dalai Lama is obstreperous and opposes all the proposed measures, considering reform to be a mistake.

(No date)

---

[1] 原文"实系传闻之误"，柔克义此处翻译有误。

蒙藏改省之入手办法（《顺天时报》第 2008 号）

日前会议政务处大臣会议改建西藏行省办法，经各王大臣议云，改建藏地行省当缓不当急。而外务部某大臣云，若不速将藏蒙改为行省，则外国以中国不遑改革，必将歧视，所以蒙藏改建行省为万不可缓之事。而改省宜先由蒙古之察哈、库伦等处入手，且于俄国通商之事宜不致棘手。至日前右丞张荫棠谒见达赖时，曾将改良藏政及开为行省各节已与达赖妥商，而达赖亦无异议，故西藏宜分作两省。惟达赖专掌宗教事宜，其振兴宗教需款不敷，当由度支部拨用，以崇尊达赖而保黄教。其他西藏政治风俗先由驻藏大臣循循改良。俟内外蒙古改建已毕，则西藏亦易办也。经各王大臣皆为赞成，不久将见逐次实行矣。

Beginning Reorganization of Mongolia and Tibet

At a meeting a few days ago of the Council of State the matter of the reorganization of Mongolia and Tibet into provinces was taken up. The Princes and Ministers of the Council thought that the division of Tibet into provinces was a matter that ought not to be undertaken in haste, and had better be postponed. One of the officials from the Foreign Office, however, said that if we did not at once set up provincial organization in Mongolia and Tibet the foreign powers, who view the situation from another angle, will think that China is delaying to effect reform. Thus the organization of provinces in Tibet and Mongolia he regarded as a matter that could not be put off. He suggested that a beginning should be made in Chahar and Urga. Moreover he thought the matter of our commercial relations with Russia was not an urgent one.

A few days ago, when the Counselor, Chang Yin-T'ang, was calling upon the Dalai Lama, he discussed with him the project of reforms in the Tibetan Government, and arranged satisfactorily with the Dalai Lama the matter of organizing provinces in Tibet. He reported that the Dalai had never held any other opinion than that Tibet ought to be divided into two provinces, but that the Dalai himself should have sole control in religious matters. It was his opinion furthermore that if funds were lacking for the promotion of interests of the Lama Church, they should be appropriated by the Imperial Treasury, in order that due honor might be given to the Dalai Lama and protection to the Yellow Church. As to political and social matters in Tibet it would rest with the Imperial Resident to initiate the discussion of such matters and to introduce the needed reforms. When Inner and Outer Mongolia shall have completed the proposed changes, it would be easy (he thought) for Tibet to take them up. Already the several Princes and Ministers of the Government are giving their assistance, and before long we shall see these changes one by one put into effect.

(No date)

Document 9 I.   Beginning Reorganization of Mongolia and Tibet.

At a meeting a few days ago of the Council of State the matter of the reorganization of Mongolia and Tibet into provinces was taken up. The Princes and Ministers of the Council thought that the division of Tibet into provinces was a matter that ought not to be undertaken in haste, and had better be postponed. One of the officials from the Foreign Office, however, said that if we did not at once set up provincial organizations in Mongolia and Tibet the foreign powers, who view the situation from another angle, will think that China is delaying to effect reform. Thus the organization of provinces in Tibet and Mongolia he regarded as a matter that could not be put off. He suggested that a beginning should be made in Chahar and Urga. Moreover he thought the matter of our commercial relations with Russia was not an urgent one.

A few days ago, when the Counselor, Chang Yin-T'ang, was calling upon the Dalai Lama, he discussed with him the project of reforms in the Tibetan Government, and arranged satisfactorily with the Dalai Lama the matter of organizing provinces in Tibet. He reported that the Dalai had never held any other opinion than that Tibet ought to be divided into two provinces, but that the Dalai himself should have sole control in religious matters. It was his opinion furthermore that if funds were lacking for the promotion of the interests of the Lama Church, they should be appropriated by the Imperial Treasury, in order that due honor might be given to the Dalai Lama and protection to the Yellow Church. As to political and social matters in Tibet it would rest with the Imperial Resident to initiate the discussion of such matters and to introduce the needed reforms. When Inner and Outer Mongolia shall have completed the proposed changes, it would be easy (he thought) for Tibet to take them up. Already the several Princes and Ministers of the Government are giving their assistance, and before long we shall see these changes one by one put into effect.

(No date)

达赖回藏期姑述

据政界人云，关于达赖回藏之期一节，大约当在来春。因政府应与达赖筹议之事非一两月间可以告竣也。

Probable date of the Dalai Lama's return to Tibet

According to statements coming from government circles, the date of the Dalai Lama's departure for Tibet will probably be some time next spring, for the matters concerning which the Government has been negotiating with him can not require more than a month or two more for settlement.

(Clipping has no date; is enclosed with one of Oct. 23, 1908)

達賴回藏期姑述 ○據政界人云關於達賴回藏之期一節大約當在來春因政府應與達賴籌議之事非一兩月間可以告竣也

```
                Group 6, Tibetan Affairs.
Document 6 C. Probable Date of the Dalai Lama's Return to Tibet.
        According to statements coming from Government Circles, the date of the
Dalai Lama's departure for Tibet will probably be some time next spring, for the
matters concerning which the Government has been negotiating with him can not
require more than a month or two more for settlement.
        (Clipping has no date; is enclosed with one of Oct.23,1908)
```

巴藏驻兵之计划

闻驻藏大臣赵季帅前曾奏请添练新军驻扎巴藏等处。现枢府诸公筹订巴藏驻兵之法，仿照戍兵归川陕甘新四省，逐年轮流派驻，现已电知川陕新甘四省照办。俟巴藏等处新军练成后再行免戍云。

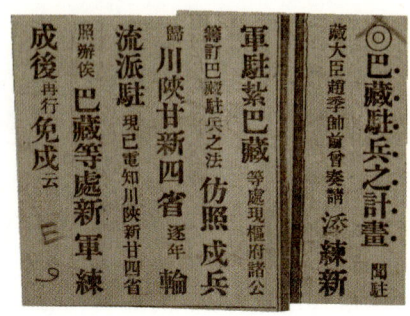

Plans Relating to Troops for Patang and Tibet

We learn that His Excellency, General Chao Chi, the Imperial Resident in Tibet, has recently memorialized requesting that a detachment from the New Army be added to the forces stationed in Patang, Tibet and that region. The responsible officers have now decided that the troops to be stationed in Patang and Tibet shall be drawn from the Frontier Guards, serving in rotation in the four provinces, Szechuen, Shensi, Kansu and Hsinchiang, but that when a force shall have been organized after the New Army model for Patang and Tibet, the Frontier Guards will be relieved.

(No date; enclosed with clipping of Oct. 23, 1908)

Group 6, Tibetan Affairs.

Document 6 E. Plans relating to Troops for Patang and Tibet.

We learn that His Excellency, General Chao Chi, the Imperial Resident in Tibet, has recently memorialized requesting that a detachment from the New Army be added to the forces stationed in Patang, Tibet and that region. The responsible officers have now decided that the troops to be stationed in Patang and Tibet shall be drawn from the Frontier Guards, serving in rotation in the four provinces Szechuen, Shensi, Kansu and Hsinchiang, but that when a force shall have been organized after the New Army model for Patang and Tibet, the Frontier Guards will be relieved.

(No date; enclosed with clipping of Oct. 23, 1908)

达赖喇嘛陛见礼节

九月廿日达赖喇嘛觐见两宫礼节见录如左：是日，皇太后升仁寿殿，召御前大臣并御前侍卫等至仁寿殿内侍立，理藩部堂官分引达赖喇嘛并通事喇嘛二名、堪布喇嘛四名进仁寿殿左门，由纳陛左阶引达赖喇嘛纳陛上侧跪，通事喇嘛二名跪于达赖喇嘛之次，堪布喇嘛四名于纳陛下侧跪。达赖喇嘛敬谨跪递佛一尊、哈达一方，御前大臣接受。堪布喇嘛四名于原跪处敬谨跪递哈达，御前侍卫接受。达赖喇嘛跪请皇太后圣安，叩谢恩赏，跪听皇太后宣谕。达赖喇嘛奏对仍由通事喇嘛递相转答。御前大臣覆"奏礼毕"，引出恭候。皇上升仁寿殿，理藩部堂官分引达赖喇嘛并通事喇嘛二名、堪布喇嘛四名进仁寿殿右门，达赖喇嘛敬谨跪递佛一尊、哈达一方；理藩部堂官引通事喇嘛二名、堪布喇嘛四名均跪于达赖喇嘛之后。堪布喇嘛四名敬谨跪递哈达，御前侍卫接受。达赖喇嘛恭请圣安，叩谢恩赏。理藩部堂官引通事喇嘛跪于达赖喇嘛之次，堪布喇嘛四名跪于达赖喇嘛之后，跪听皇上宣谕。达赖喇嘛奏对仍由通事喇嘛递相转答。御前大臣覆"奏毕礼毕"，引出。

Ceremony at the Audience Granted to the Dalai Lama

On the 20th of the Ninth Moon (Oct.14th, 1908) the Dalai Lama will have audience of Their Imperial Majesties, the Empress Dowager and the Emperor. The ceremony will be as follows:

On the day stated H.I.M. the Empress Dowager will ascend the throne in the Jen

Rockhill Papers.

Translations from the Chinese.

GROUP 6 - Tibetan Affairs.

Document, 6 A. Ceremony at the Audience granted to the Dalai Lama.

On the 20th. of the Ninth Moon (Oct. 14th. 1908) the Dalai Lama will have audience of Their Imperial Majesties, the Empress Dowager and the Emperor. The ceremony will be as follows:-

On the day stated H.I.M. the Empress Dowager will ascend the throne in the Jen Shou Tien and will summon the Ministers of the Presence, as well as the Commander of the Imperial Body Guard, to the Jen Shou Tien, to be in attendance upon the officers of the Ministry of Dependencies, who will introduce the Dalai Lama together with the two lama interpreters and the four lama abbots. They will lead them into the Jen Shou Tien through the eastern opening of the doorway. The Master of Ceremonies will then ascend the throne dais with the Dalai Lama, going up by the eastern steps. The Master of Ceremonies will then step to one side and kneel. The two lama interpreters and the four lama abbots will also kneel beside and below the Master of Ceremonies.

The Dalai Lama will reverently and respectfully kneel and present a Buddhist image and a scarf. The Minister of the Presence will receive them. The four abbots will pay their reverence in the place where they are kneeling, and will present scarfs. The Commander of the Body Guard will receive them.

The Dalai Lama, kneeling, will express a wish for the health of H.I.M. the Empress Dowager and will kotow as a manifestation of his gratitude to her for the favor shown in bestowing the audience.

The two lama interpreters will translate the commands of the Empress Dowager to the Dalai Lama and his responses to the Throne.

Shou Tien and will summon the Ministers of the Presence, as well as the commands of the Imperial Body Guard, to the Jen Shou Tien, to be in attendance upon the officers of the Ministry of Dependencies, who will introduce the Dalai Lama together with the two lama interpreters and the four lama abbots. They will lead them into the Jen Shou Tien through the eastern opening of the doorway. The Master of Ceremonies will then ascend the throne dais with the Dalai Lama, going up by the eastern steps. The Master of Ceremonies will then step to one side and kneel. The two lama interpreters and the four lama abbots will also kneel beside and below the Master of Ceremonies[1].

The Dalai Lama will reverently and respectfully kneel and present a Buddhist image and a scarf. The Minister of the Presence will receive them. The four abbots will pay their reverence in the place where they are kneeling, and will present scarfs. The Commander of the Body Guard will receive them.

The Dalai Lama, kneeling, will express a wish for the health of H.I.M. the Empress Dowager and will kotow as a manifestation of his gratitude to her for the favor shown in bestowing the audience.

The two lama interpreters will translate the commands of the Empress Dowager to the Dalai Lama and his responses to the Throne.

The Minister of the Presence will then request that the audience be closed, and will conduct the guests out of the audience chamber to await reverently the entrance to the Jen Shou Tien of H.I.M. the Emperor.

The officers of the Ministry of Dependencies will separately lead into the Jen Shou Tien the Dalai Lama, the two lama interpreters and the four abbots. They will go in by the western opening of the doorway. The Dalai Lama will reverently and respectfully kneel and present to His Majesty a Buddhist image and a scarf. The officers of the Ministry of Dependencies, conducting the two lama interpreters and the four abbots, will cause them to kneel behind the Dalai Lama. The four abbots, while kneeling, will reverently present their scarfs, which the Commander of the Body Guard will receive.

The Dalai Lama will ask after the health of H.I.M. the Emperor and kotow to him as an expression of his thankfulness for the favor of the audience. The officers of the Ministry of Dependencies will bring the two lama interpreters close to the Dalai Lama.

---

[1] 柔克义错误地理解了原文"纳陛"的含义，将其误译为"Master of Ceremonies"。

6A   2

    The Minister of the Presence will then request that the audience be closed, and will conduct the guests out of the audience chamber to await reverently the entrance to the Jen Shou Tien of H.I.M. the Emperor.

    The officers of the Ministry of Dependencies will separately lead into the Jen Shou Tien the Dalai Lama, the two lama interpreters and the four abbots. They will go in by the western opening of the doorway. The Dalai Lama will reverently and respectfully kneel and present to His Majesty a Buddhist image and a scarf. The officers of the Ministry of Dependencies, conducting the two lama interpreters and the four abbots, will cause them to kneel behind the Dalai Lama. The four abbots, while kneeling, will reverently present their scarfs, which the Commander of the Body Guard will receive.

    The Dalai Lama will ask after the health of H.I.M. the Emperor and kotow to him as an expression of his thankfulness for the favor of the audience. The officers of the Ministry of Dependencies will bring the two lama interpreters close to the Dalai Lama. The four abbots will continue kneeling behind the Dalai Lama. All will reverently listen to His Majesty's commands, to which the Dalai Lama will reply. The two lama interpreters will translate the conversation. After this the Minister of the Presence will request that the audience be closed, and will conduct the visitors to the outside.

The four abbots will continue kneeling behind the Dalai Lama. All will reverently listen to His Majesty's commands, to which the Dalai Lama will reply. The two lama interpreters will translate the conversation. After this the Minister of the Presence will request that the audience be closed, and will conduct the visitors to the outside.

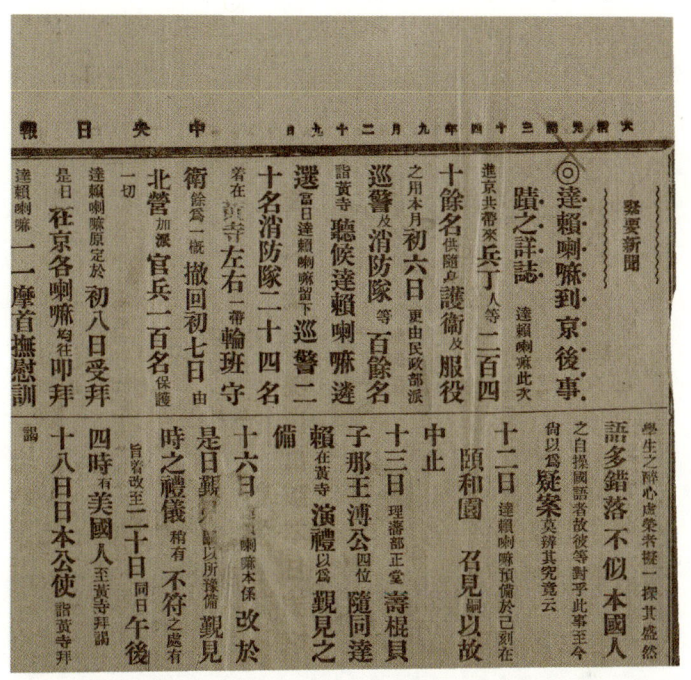

达赖喇嘛到京后事迹之详志（《中央日报》大清光绪三十四年九月二十九日　紧要新闻）

达赖喇嘛此次进京共带来兵丁人等二百四十余名，供随身护卫及服役之用。本月初六日更由民政部派巡警及消防队等百余名诣黄寺听候达赖喇嘛遴选。当日达赖喇嘛留下巡警二十名、消防队二十四名，着在黄寺左右一带轮班守卫，余为一概撤回。初七日由北营加派官兵一百名保护一切。达赖喇嘛原定于初八日受拜，是日，在京各喇嘛均往叩拜，达赖喇嘛一一摩首抚慰训示多词，喇嘛等皆罗拜谢恩，欢呼而退。初十日下午三句钟，理藩部右侍达寿前往黄寺拜见达赖喇嘛，历二小时许始出。是日傍晚，有着西服者二人至黄寺徘徊门际，意似欲入而恐见摈于门人者，逡巡数十分皆怏怏而去。或云此系某国新闻社特派员，未察确否。闻其临去时二人相对操华语，故高其声。当时望者疑系留学生之醉心虚荣者，拟一探其盛。然语多错落，不似本国人之自操国语者，故彼等对乎此事至今尚以为疑案，莫辨其究竟云。十二日，达赖喇嘛预备于巳刻在颐和园召见，嗣以故中止。十三日，理藩部正堂、寿昆贝子、那王、溥公四位随同达赖在黄寺演礼，以为觐见之备。十六日，达赖喇嘛本系改于是日觐见，嗣以所预备觐见时之礼仪稍有不符之处，有旨着改至二十日。同日午后四时，有美国人至黄寺拜谒。十八日，日本公使诣黄寺拜谒。二十日早四点，达赖喇嘛由黄寺前往颐和园觐见，下午一时归（详见前

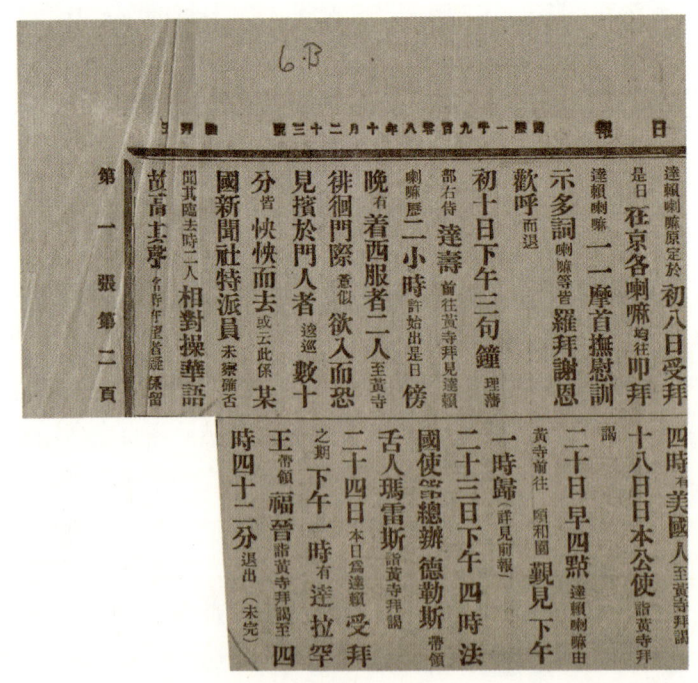

Rockhill Papers.

Translations from the Chinese.

GROUP 6 - Tibetan Affairs.

Document 6 B. A Diary of Events connected with the Visit of the Dalai Lama. I.

On the occasion of the visit of the Dalai Lama to Peking he was escorted by 240 soldiers as a body guard for his protection and to wait upon him. On the 6th. inst. (Sept. 30th. 1908) the Ministry of the Interior substituted policemen and firemen to the number of over a hundred persons, who were sent to the Yellow Temple to be under the orders of the Dalai Lama. The latter on the same day selected twenty of the policemen and twenty-four of the firemen, and divided them into two shifts to take turns in watching over the Yellow Temple. The remainder were all sent back.

On the 7th. inst. the Northern Barracks sent in addition one hundred officers and men to furnish protection. According to the original plan of the Dalai Lama the 8th. inst. was fixed upon as a day to receive visitors. On that day all the lamas in Peking called and kotowed to His Holiness. He placed his hand upon them one by one and blessed them, addressing a few words to them. The lamas, kneeling in a circle around him, worshipped him, and after thanking him for the gracious summons departed.

On the 10th. at 3 p.m. Ta-Shou, the Second Vice Minister of Dependencies, called at the Yellow Temple to pay his respects and was received in audience. Only after two hours was he permitted to retire.

The same day near evening two representatives of a foreign newspaper were seen walking to and fro near the entrance to the Yellow Temple, as if greatly desirous of going in, but, perhaps because they saw persons driven away from the gate, they were deterred, and after several minutes they walked rapidly away. It is reported that these men were specially appointed representatives of the Press Association of a certain country. We have not discovered whether or not this is true. We learn that just as they went away they talked to one another in Chinese in loud tones. The watch on duty at the time thought that they were silly, drunken students, who had come to

报）。二十三日下午四时，法国使馆总办德勒斯带领舌人玛雷斯诣黄寺拜谒。二十四日，本日为达赖受拜之期，下午一时，有达拉罕王带领福晋诣黄寺拜谒，至四时四十二分退出。

A Diary of Events Connected with the Visit of the Dalai Lama. I.

On the occasion of the visit of the Dalai Lama to Peking he was escorted by 240 soldiers as a body guard for his protection and to wait upon him. On the 6th. inst. (Sept. 30th, 1908) the Ministry of the Interior substituted policemen and firemen to the number of over a hundred persons, who were sent to the Yellow Temple to be under the orders of the Dalai Lama. The latter on the same day selected twenty of the policemen and twenty-four of the firemen, and divided them into two shifts to take turns in watching over the Yellow Temple. The remainder were all sent back.

On the 7th. inst. the Northern Barracks sent in addition one hundred officers and men to furnish protection. According to the original plan of the Dalai Lama the 8th. inst. was fixed upon as a day to receive visitors. On that day all the lamas in Peking called and kotowed to His Holiness. He placed his hand upon them one by one and blessed them, addressing a few words to them. The lamas, kneeling in a circle around him, worshipped him, and after thanking him for the gracious summons departed.

On the 10th. at 3 p.m. Ta-Shou, the Second Vice Minister of Dependencies, called

---

6 B   2

see what they could discover, but their speech was full of errors and not like the talk of Chinese among themselves, so that what they had to do with affairs is still a matter of doubt and no investigation has been made.

On the 12th. inst. the Dalai Lama was making ready for an audience at the Summer Palace at 9 a.m. but all preparations were suddenly stopped. On the 13th. the Minister of Dependencies, together with Prince Shou-Kun and Prince Na and Duke Pu, four in all, went together to the Yellow Temple to rehearse the ceremony in preparation for the audience. The Dalai Lama had at first changed the date of the audience to the 16th., but later because the ceremony as arranged did not suit in some respects an imperial edict appeared changing the date to the 20th. On the 16th. also, at 4 p.m. certain Americans called to pay their respects. On the 18th. the Japanese Minister called.

At four o'clock on the morning of the 20th. the Dalai Lama left the Yellow Temple for the Summer Palace, where he was received in audience. At one p.m. he returned. (An account of the audience has already been given in an earlier issue.)

On the 23d. at 4 p.m. M. Te-le-ssu, of the French Legation, accompanied by the Interpreter, M. Maurice, called at the Yellow Temple.

The 24th. was the Dalai Lama's reception day. At 1 p.m. His Highness Prince Talahan, with the Princess, went to the Yellow Temple. They remained until 4:40 p.m. when they went away.   (Oct. 23,1908)

(To be continued.)

at the Yellow Temple to pay his respects and was received in audience. Only after two hours was he permitted to retire.

The same day near evening two representatives of a foreign newspaper were seen walking to and fro near the entrance to the Yellow Temple, as if greatly desirous of going in, but, perhaps because they saw persons driven away from the gate, they were deterred, and after several minutes they walked rapidly away. It is reported that these men were specially appointed representatives of the Press Association of a certain country. We have not discovered whether or not this is true. We learn that just as they went away they talked to one another in Chinese in loud tones. The watch on duty at the time thought that they were silly, drunken students[1], who had come to see what they could discover, but their speech was full of errors and not like the talk of Chinese among themselves, so that what they had to do with affairs is still a matter of doubts and no investigation has been made.

On the 12th. inst. the Dalai Lama was making ready for an audience at the Summer Palace at 9 a.m. but all preparation was suddenly stopped. On the 13th. the Minister of Dependencies, together with Prince Shou-Kun and Prince Na and Duke Pu, four in all, went together to the Yellow Temple to rehearse the ceremony in preparation for the audience. The Dalai Lama had at first changed the date of the audience to the 16th, but later because the ceremony as arranged did not suit in some respects an imperial edict appeared changing the date to the 20th. On the 16th. also, at 4 p.m. certain Americans called to pay their respects. On the 18th. the Japanese Minister called.

At four o'clock on the morning of the 20th. the Dalai Lama left the Yellow Temple for the Summer Palace, where he was received in audience. At one p.m. he returned. (An account of the audience has already been given in an earlier issue.)

On the 23rd. at 4 p.m. M. Te-le-ssu, of the French Legation, accompanied by the Interpreter, M. Maurice, called at the Yellow Temple.

The 24th. was the Dalai Lama's reception day. At 1 p.m. His Highness Prince Talahan, with the Princess, went to the Yellow Temple. They remained until 4:40 p.m. when they went away.

(Oct. 23, 1908)
To be continued

---

[1] 此处柔克义误译了原文"醉心虚荣"的意思。

157

达赖喇嘛到京后事迹之详志（《中央日报》大清光绪三十四年九月三十日 紧要新闻）

本月二十三日，达赖喇嘛处有法国使馆二人来见，已志昨报。兹探得当日达赖喇嘛接该法人名片时即点首示意令传见，嗣复回顾其最亲信之侍者某，踌躇数分之久，忽如有所触，遂令传命挡驾。是以当日法人虽已入黄寺，并未得面谒达赖喇嘛云。

二十五日十二时，外务部张荫棠参议诣黄寺拜谒，三时二十分顷退出。又一时三十分，雍和宫栋克尔至黄寺，二时十五分顷退出。又二时三十五分，葡国钦差柏罗德带领汉文参赞面谒达赖，当时赏赐该钦差藏枣石榴各一盘，会谈之际双方辞色皆甚形殷恳，惟以言语不通，动辄皆须通译，似甚不满意者。并闻葡使自称不通贵国语言，深以为恨。达赖喇嘛答以余意亦然。坐谈既久，适侍者以名刺来云，更有一外国人求面谒者，葡使遂匆匆辞出，时正午后三时二十五分。葡使退后而所谓求面谒之外国人遂入坐，谈至五时前十分始退。据闻此系美人，日前曾来此一次者。并闻当葡使出而美人入之际，同时更有英国二等翻译官梅尔斯及武官哈阿墩布诣黄寺求见未得云。

二十六日午后一时，英国钦使朱尔典率三等参赞阿尔正，翻译甘伯乐、梅尔斯，商务大臣谢莫，武官白伯乐，大夫德来戈并学生琢乃思、毕月、南卜氏、哲氏等四人诣黄寺谒见达赖喇嘛，当时赏赐钦使西藏枣、金丝枣各一盘。四时顷皆告辞退出。

Diary of Events Connected with the Visit of the Dalai Lama (Continued)

On the 23rd inst. (Oct. 17) two gentlemen from the French legation called upon the Dalai Lama, as already reported in yesterday's issue. We now learn by enquiry that on the said day when the Dalai Lama received the gentlemen's cards, he nodded his head and directed that they be received. After this he turned again to give attention to his most confidential follower. Some moments passed causing embarrassments to

Group 8, Tibetan affairs.   1

Document 8 A.   Diary of Events Connected with the Visit of the Dalai Lama.(Continued

     On the 23d. inst. (Oct. 17) two gentlemen from the French Legation called upon the Dalai Lama, as already reported in yesterday's issue. We now learn by enquiry that on the said day when the Dalai Lama received the gentlemen's cards, he nodded his head and directed that they be received. After this he turned again to give attention to his most confidential follower. Some moments passed causing embarrassment to the visitors, when another message came from the Dalai Lama, as if offense had been given, saying that he was engaged. Thus the Frenchmen, although admitted to the Yellow Temple, did not see His Holiness.
     On the 25th. at noon Chang Yin-T'ang, Counsellor of the Foreign Office, went in person to the Yellow Temple and had an interview which lasted until twenty minutes past three, when he withdrew.
     At 1:30 p.m. the Tongkhor of the Yung Ho Kung, arrived at the Yellow Temple and at 2:15 went away. At 2:35 the Portuguese Minister, Po-lo-ti, called with his Chinese Secretary and had an audience. The Dalai Lama presented him with a plate of Tibetan jujubes and one of pomgranates. Both parties appeared to be anxious to speak, but, since they did not understand one anothers language, there was no way of starting a conversation. The interpreter did not seem to be quite satisfactory. We learn also that the Portuguese Minister said:-"I am ashamed that I cannot speak your honorable tongue." The Dalai Lama expressed similar feeling with regard to Portuguese. After a few moments a servant came in with a card and said that another foreign gentleman had called and asked for an audience. The Portuguese Minister at once took his departure. It was then 3:25 p.m. The gentleman announced entered and remained until ten minutes of five, when he took his leave. We hear that this was an American who had called once before. We hear also that when the Portuguese Minister took his leave and the American entered, two Englishmen also called at the same time; Mr. Mayers, the Chinese Secretary of the British Legation and the Military Attache, Ho-o-tun-pu. They sought an interview but failed to get it.
     On the 26th. in the afternoon at one o'clock Sir John Jordan, the British Minister, called with the Third Secretary, O-erh-cheng, Mr. Campbell the Interpreter Mr. Mayers and the Commercial Attache, Hsieh-mo and the following military officers: Pai-po-lo, Ta-fu, and Te-lai-kuo. Beside these there were four student interpreters: Messrs. Jones, Pi-yueh, Nan-pu-shi, and Che-shih. They had audience of the Dalai Lama, who presented the Minister with Tibetan dates and golden-thread dates, one dish of each. At four o'clock they took their leave.
                      (October 24, 1908)

the visitors, when another message came from the Dalai Lama, as if offense had been given, saying that he was engaged. Thus the Frenchmen, although admitted to the Yellow Temple, did not see His Holiness.

On the 25th. at noon Chang Yin-T'ang, counselor of the Foreign Office, went in person to the Yellow Temple and had an interview which lasted until twenty minutes past three, when he withdrew.

At 1:30 p.m. the Tongkhor of the Yung Ho Kung arrived at the Yellow Temple and at 2:15 went away. At 2:35 the Portuguese Minster, Po-lo-ti, called with his Chinese Secretary and had an audience. The Dalai Lama presented him with a plate of Tibetan jujubes and one of the pomegranates. Both parties appears to be anxious to speak, but, since they did not understand one another's language, there was no way of starting a conversation. The interpreter did not seem to be quite satisfactory. We learn also that the Portuguese Minster said "I am ashamed that I cannot speak your honorable tongue." The Dalai Lama expressed similar feeling with regard to Portuguese. After a few moments a servant came in with a card and said that another foreign gentleman had called and asked for an audience. The Portuguese Minster at once took his departure. It was then 3:25 p.m. The gentleman announced entered and remained until ten minutes of five, when he took his leave. We hear that this was an American who had called once before. We hear also that when the Portuguese Minster took his leave and the American entered, two Englishmen also called at the same time; Mr. Mayers the Chinese Secretary of the British Legation and the Military Attache, Ho-o-tun-pu. They sought an interview but failed to get it.

On the 26th. in the afternoon at one o'clock Sir John Jordan, the British Minister, called with the third Secretary, O-erh-cheng, Mr. Campbell the Interpreter, Mr. Mayers and the Commercial Attache, Hsieh-mo and the following military officers, Pai-po-lo, Ta-fu, and Te-lai-kuo. Beside these there were four student interpreters; Messrs, Jones, Pi-yueh, Nan-pu-shi, and Che-shih. They had audience of the Dalai Lama, who presented the Minister with Tibetan dates and Golden-thread dates, one dish of each. At four o'clock they took their leave.

(October 24, 1908)

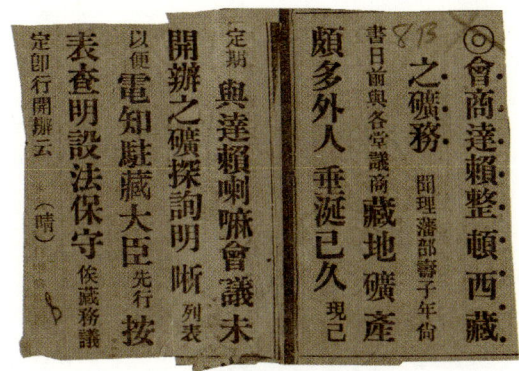

会商达赖整顿西藏之矿务

闻理藩部寿子年尚书日前与各堂议商，藏地矿产颇多，外人垂涎已久，现已定期与达赖喇嘛会议，未开办之矿，探询明晰列表，以便电知驻藏大臣先行按表查明，设法保守，俟藏务议定即行开办云。

Conference on Mining Regulations for Tibet

We hear that the Minister of Dependencies, H.E. Shou Tzu-Nien, a few days ago consulted with the other Minister of Cabinet concerning mining regulations for Tibet. The mouths of many foreigners have long been watering for these. A date has now been fixed for consultation with the Dalai Lama concerning the matter. A careful survey is to be made before opening any mines, and a tabulated list is to be prepared. The Imperial Resident in Tibet will be instructed by telegraph to make first an investigation in accordance with the tabulated list and suggest a method of operation, one that will protect our interests. He must then await a decision in regard to Tibetan Affairs before undertaking any mining.

(No date)

Document 8 B.   Conference on Mining Regulations for Tibet.

We hear that the Minister of Dependencies, H.E. Shou Tzu-Nien, a few days ago consulted with the other Ministers of the Cabinet concerning mining regulations for Tibet. The mouths of many foreigners have long been watering for these. A date has now been fixed for consultation with the Dalai Lama concerning the matter. A careful survey is to be made before opening any mines, and a tabulated list is to be prepared. The Imperial Resident in Tibet will be instructed by telegraph to make first an investigation in accordance with the tabulated list and suggest a method of operation, one that will protect our interests. He must then await a decision in regard to Tibetan affairs before undertaking any mining.

(No date)

161

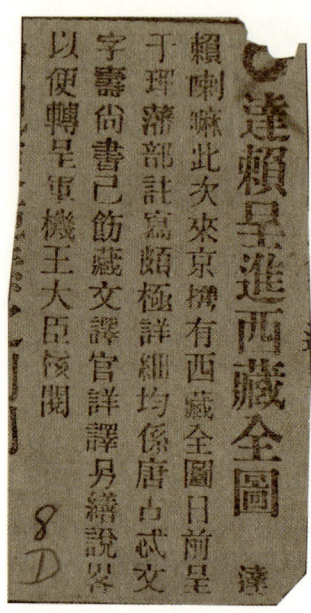

达赖呈进西藏全图

达赖喇嘛此次来京携有西藏全图，日前呈于理藩部注写颇极详细，均系唐古忒文字，寿尚书已饬藏文译官详译，另缮说略，以便转呈军机王大臣核阅。

The Dalai Lama Presents a Map of Tibet

The Dalai Lama, on the occasion of his present visit to Peking, brought with him a complete map of Tibet which a few days ago he presented to the Ministry of Dependencies. The map has very detailed information in the Tangut script. Minister Shou has already given orders to the Tibetan interpreters to translate the same and to add also an explanation, so that it may be transmitted to the Princes and Ministers of the Grand Council for consideration.

(No date)

Document 8 D.   The Dalai Lama Presents a Map of Tibet.

The Dalai Lama, on the occasion of his present visit to Peking, brought with him a complete map of Tibet which a few days ago he presented to the Ministry of Dependencies. The map has very detailed information in the Tangut script. Minister Shou has already given orders to the Tibetan interpreters to translate the same and to add also an explanation, so that it may be transmitted to the Princes and Ministers of the Grand Council for consideration.

(No date)

（三）圣谕和奏折等资料

　　柔克义搜集了 1908 年有关达赖喇嘛觐见帝后的圣谕和奏折，这些圣谕和奏折主要刊登在当时的《政府官报》上，柔克义将其翻译成英文，作为美国驻华公使馆的公文发回美国国务院，其中详细记载了达赖喇嘛向光绪皇帝和慈禧太后跪拜的情况。

哈佛大学图书馆藏柔克义档案 MS AM2122（93）
该件档案为《奏定接待十三世达赖喇嘛节略》译文，档案中无中文原文，为读者对照阅读方便，现将中文原文补录于此。

奏定接待十三世达赖喇嘛节略 [1]

接待达赖喇嘛节略

——由山西巡抚传旨，召达赖来京陛见。

——山西巡抚遵派大员赴五台山，询定达赖启程日期，先行电奏。

——由理藩部会同内务府预勘黄寺房屋，估计修理，并将铺陈器具酌量
　　置备。

——山西巡抚遵旨派文武大员自五台山沿途照料，至山西省城后，换坐
　　火车来京。

——达赖行抵山西省时，请旨派山西巡抚在省城外迎迓劳问。

——预计行近保定日期，请先旨简派御前大臣一人赴保定迎迓劳问。

——驻扎保定陆军各营，出队在车站排列迎送。

---

[1] 中国第一历史档案馆、中国藏学研究中心：《清末十三世达赖喇嘛档案史料选编》，中国藏学出版社 2002 年版，第 138—139 页。

——保定布政使以下各地方官，同在车站迎送。

——行抵京城，理藩部堂官、内务府大臣、步军统领、顺天府府尹，暨在京首领各喇嘛，同赴车站迎迓。

——民政部派巡警队暨乐队在车站迎迓，并派巡警队护送至黄寺。

——达赖抵黄寺后，由陆军部酌调营队驻扎保护。

——每日供给，由理藩部、内务府妥定章程，会同派员经理。

——达赖抵京之日，皇太后、皇上赏给鞍马、尺头、银两等件。

——由理藩部请旨，定期召见达赖，先期在黄寺演礼。陛见之日，达赖进殿门，皇上起立。达赖恭请圣安，并叩谢恩赏，皇上立受，问候。御座侧设矮床，为达赖座。皇上升座，宣温谕，赐达赖坐，赐茶。达赖面奏藏中情形。其详细节目暨赐予贡献各典礼，由理藩部另拟请旨。

——是日，皇太后、皇上赏朝珠、玉佩、佛帽、斗篷、衣服、哈达等件。

——内务府请旨定期赐宴，其礼如紫光阁赐宴例，惟为达赖设矮床，侧座。

——是日，皇太后、皇上赏金银器、玉器、茶叶、食物等件。

——达赖回藏有期，皇太后、皇上赏马匹、银两、毛皮、缎匹等件。

——遇有恩赏，由理藩部代奏谢恩；如蒙面赏，达赖叩首谢恩。

——出京之日，请旨派御前大臣一人，暨理藩部尚书、内务府大臣，择地设饯。

——理藩部堂官、内务府大臣等送至车站，如来时仪。

——请旨派御前大臣一人送至保定。

——军队、巡警队及所过地方各官迎送，如来时仪。

——沿途各督、抚、将军、都统派文武大员护送照料供应。

2

AMERICAN LEGATION,
PEKING, CHINA.　　Augt 1908

Translation.

Rules for the reception of the Dalai Lama sent from the Grand
Council to the Board of Dependencies, the Board of the Interior
and the Comptrollers of the Imperial Household.

1.　The Governor of Shansi shall summon the Dalai Lama to an
Imperial Audience.

2.　The Governor of Shansi shall send a high official to ask
the Dalai Lama the date of his setting out upon his journey and
shall notify the Court by telegraph.

3.　The Board of Dependencies (Li Fan Pu) in connection with the Imperial
Household Department shall arrange the preparation of the
Huang Ssŭ and prepare the ceremonial presents to be offered.

4.　The Governor of Shansi shall send high civil and military
offials to escort the Dalai Lama from Wu T'ai Shan to Tai Yŭan
Fu, where he will take the train.

5.　The Governor of Shansi shall receive the Dalai Lama outside the city gate of Thai Yŭan Fu.

6.　The Emperor will be requested to send some one immediately
connected with the Court to Paoting Fu to greet the Dalai Lama
on his arrival at that place.

7.　All the troops at Paoting Fu will be drawn up at the
Railway Station to receive the Dalai Lama.

8.　All the officials at Paoting Fu, from the Provincial
Treasurer downward, will pay their respects to the Dalai Lama
at the Railway Station.

9.　The higher officials of the Board of Dependances, and of
the Imperial Household Department, (Wei wu Fu) the Commandants of the
Army, the Governor of Peking and the Head Lamas will receive the
Dalai Lama at the Railway Station of Peking.

10.　The City Police Department will send a company of Police
and a Band of Music to meet the Dalai at the Railway Station
and the Police will escort him to the Huang Ssŭ.

11.　The Board of War will detail a company of soldiers to
guard the Dalai during his residence at the Huang Ssŭ.

American Legation

Peking, China

August, 1908

Rules for the reception of the Dalai Lama sent from the Grand Council to the Board of Dependencies, the Board of Interior and Comptrollers of Imperial Household

1. The Governor of Shanxi shall summon the Dalai Lama to an imperial audience.

2. The Governor of Shanxi shall send a high official to ask the Dalai Lama the date of his setting up upon his journey and shall notify the court by telegraph.

3. The Board of Dependencies (Li-Fan-Pu) in connection with the Imperial Household Department shall arrange the preparation of the Huang-Ssu and prepare the ceremonial presents to be offered.

4. The Governor of Shanxi shall send high civil and military officials to escort the Dalai Lama from Wu T'ai Shan to T'ai Yuan Fu, where he would take the train.

5. The Governor of Shanxi shall receive the Dalai Lama outside the gate of T'ai Yuan Fu.

6. The Emperor will be requested to send someone immediately connected with the court to Paoting Fu to greet the Dalai Lama on his arrival on that place.

7. All the troops at Paoting Fu will be drawn up at the railway station to receive the Dalai Lama.

8. All the officials at Paoting Fu, from the Provincial Treasurer downward, will pay their respect to the Dalai Lama at the railway station.

9. The higher officials of the Board of Dependencies, and of the Imperial Household Department, the commandant of the army, the Governor of Peking, and the Head Lamas will receive the Dalai Lama at the Railway Station of Peking.

10. The City Police Department will send a company of police and a Band of Music

AMERICAN LEGATION.
PEKING, CHINA

Rules for the Reception of the Dalai Lama

Page 2.

12. The supplies will be furnished by the Board of Dependencies and the Imperial Household Department according to rules to be drawn up by them.

13. After the arrival of the Dalai Lama at Peking the Emperor and the Empress Dowager will make him presents of saddle horses, rolls of silk etc.

14. The Board of Dependencies will memorialize the Throne asking that a date may be fixed for an Imperial Audience. The Dalai will familirize himself with the ceremonies beforehand, after his arrival at the Huang Ssu. For the Imperial Audience he will enter the Palace by the Hsien-Men. The Emperor will greet him standing. The Dalai will respectfully greet the Emperor and kotow to thank His Majesty for the Imperial gifts. The Emperor will receive this standing and ask after his health. A low couch shall be prepared beside the throne on which the Dalai may sit. After the Emperor has taken his seat he will invite the Dalai to be seated and will give him tea, after which they will discuss Tibetan affairs together. The presents to be exchanged will be determined by the Board of Dependencies.

15. On the same day the Empress Dowager and the Emperor will present dynastic pearls, jade pendants, Buddistic hats, capes, clothing, hats, etc.

16. The Imperial Household Department will memorialize asking the time to be fixed for a banquet. This shall be according to the rules of the Tzu-kuang-ko banquets, with a low couch on which the Dalai shall sit.

17. On the same day the Empress Dowager and the Emperor will present the Dalai with silver and jade utensils, tea, food, etc.

18. When the time is fixed for the Dalai's return to Tibet, the Empress Dowager and the Emperor will present him with horses, silver, furs, satin, etc.

19. The Board of Dependencies will return thanks for the Im-

AMERICAN LEGATION.
PEKING, CHINA.

Rules for the Reception of the Dalai Lama.

Page 3.

perial gifts. If the Dalai does this in person, he will perform the kotow.

20. On the day when the Dalai leaves Peking a memorial will request that a special envoy be appointed, as well as the President of the Board of Dependences and the Superintendent of the Imperial Household, to arrange for a farewell banquet.

21. The higher officials of the Board of Dependences and the Imperial Household will escort the Dalai to the Railway Station with similar ceremonies, as on his arrival.

21. A special envoy shall escort the Dalai to Paoting Fu.

22. Officials, soldiers etc. will show him the same attentions as when he came to Peking.

23. Viceroys, Governors, Military officials etc. on the route of the Dalai's return journey will show him attentions and give him protection.

to meet the Dalai at the Railway Station and the police will escort him to the Huang Ssu.

11. The Board of War will detail a company of soldiers to guard the Dalai during his residence at Huang Ssu.

12. The supplies will be furnished by the Board of Dependencies and the Imperial Household Department, according to rules to be drawn up by them.

13. After the arrival of the Dalai Lama at Peking the Emperor and Empress Dowager will make him presents of saddles horses, rolls of silk etc.

14. The Board of Dependencies will memorialize the Throne asking that a date may be fixed for an imperial audience. The Dalai will familiarize himself with the ceremonies beforehand, after his arrival at Huang Ssu. For the imperial audience he will enter the palace door, and the Emperor will greet him standing. The Dalai will respectfully greet the Emperor and kotow (叩首) to thank His Majesty for the imperial gifts. The Emperor will receive this standing, and ask after his health. A low couch shall be prepared beside the throne on which the Dalai may sit. After the Emperor has taken his seat he will invite the Dalai to be seated and will give him tea, after which they will discuss Tibetan affairs together. The presents to be exchanged will be determined by the Board of Dependencies.

15. On the same day the Empress Dowager and Emperor will present "dynastic" pearls, jade pendants, Buddhistic hats, capes and clothing, "Ha-ta", etc.

16. The Imperial Household Department will memorialize asking the time to be fixed for a banquet. This shall be according to the rules of the Tzu-kuang-ko banquet, with a low couch on which the Dalai Lama shall sit.

17. On the same day the Empress Dowager and the Emperor will present the Dalai with silver and jade utensils, tea, food, etc.

18. When the time is fixed for the Dalai's return to Tibet, the Empress Dowager and the Emperor will present him with horses, silver, furs, satin, etc.

19. The Board of Dependencies will return thanks for the imperial gifts. If the Dalai does this in person, he will perform the kotow.

20. On the day the Dalai Lama leaves Peking a memorial will request that a special envoy be appointed, as well as the President of the Board of Dependencies, and the superintendent of the Imperial Household, will arrange for a farewell banquet.

21. The higher officials of the Board of Dependencies and the Imperial Household will escort the Dalai to the Railway Station with ceremonies, as on his arrival.

22. A special envoy shall escort the Dalai to Pao T'ing Fu.

23. Officials, soldiers, etc. will show him the same attentions, as when he came to Peking.

24. Viceroys, Governors, Military officials etc. on the route of the Dalai's return journey will show him the attentions and give him protection.

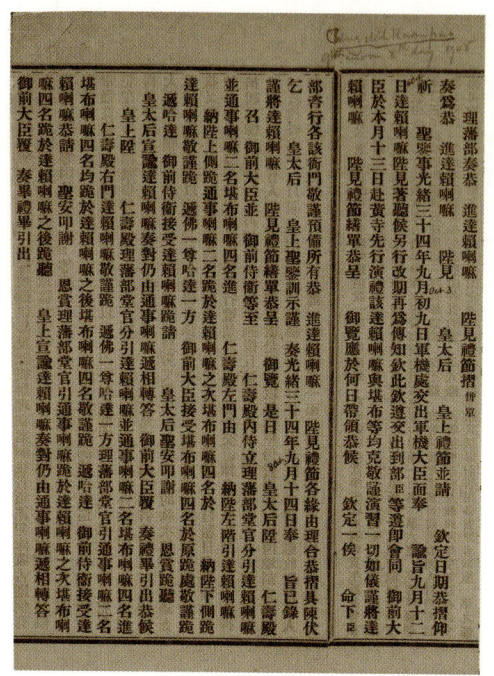

理藩部奏恭进达赖喇嘛陛见礼节折

奏为恭进达赖喇嘛陛见皇太后、皇上礼节，并请钦定日期，恭折仰祈圣鉴事。光绪三十四年九月初九日军机处交出军机大臣面奉，谕旨九月十二日达赖喇嘛陛见，着听候另行改期，再为传知，钦此。钦遵交出到部，臣等遵即会同御前大臣于本月十三日赴黄寺先行演礼，该达赖喇嘛与堪布等均克敬谨演习，一切如仪，谨将达赖喇嘛陛见礼节缮单恭呈御览。应于何日带领恭候钦定，一俟命下，臣部咨行各该衙门敬谨预备。所有恭进达赖喇嘛陛见礼节，各缘由理合恭折具陈，伏乞皇太后、皇上圣鉴训示。谨奏光绪三十四年九月十四日奉旨已录，谨将恭进达赖喇嘛陛见礼节缮单恭呈御览。是日，皇太后升仁寿殿，召御前大臣并御前侍卫等至仁寿殿内侍立，理藩部堂官分引达赖喇嘛并通事喇嘛二名、堪布喇嘛四名进仁寿殿左门，由纳陛左阶引达赖喇嘛纳陛上侧跪，通事喇嘛二名跪于达赖喇嘛之次，堪布喇嘛四名于纳陛下侧跪。达赖喇嘛敬谨跪递佛一尊、哈达一方，御前大臣接受；堪布喇嘛四名于原跪处敬谨跪递哈达，御前侍卫接受；达赖喇嘛跪请皇太后圣安，叩谢恩赏，跪听皇太后宣谕。达赖喇嘛奏对，仍由通事喇嘛递相转答。御前大臣覆：奏礼毕，引出恭候。皇上升仁寿殿，理藩部堂官分引达赖喇嘛并通事喇嘛二名、堪布喇嘛四名进仁寿殿右门，达赖喇嘛敬谨跪递佛一尊、哈达一方。理藩部堂官引通事喇嘛二名、堪布喇嘛四名均跪于达赖喇嘛之后。堪布喇嘛四名敬谨跪递哈达，御前侍卫接受。达赖喇嘛恭请圣安，叩谢恩赏。理藩部堂官引通事喇嘛跪于达赖喇嘛之次，堪布喇嘛四名跪于达赖喇嘛之后，跪听皇上宣谕。达赖喇嘛奏对，仍由通事喇嘛递相转答。御前大臣覆"奏毕礼毕"引出。

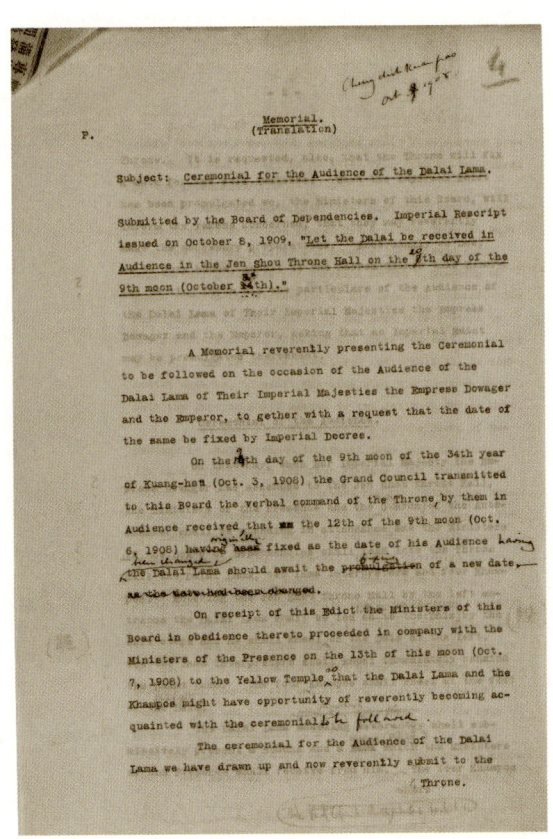

交旨

九月二十五日交理藩部、军机大臣面奉谕旨：达赖喇嘛着于入宴坐次跪迎跪送，钦此。同日交理藩部、礼部、军机大臣面奉谕旨：达赖喇嘛祝嘏着于王大臣行礼后，在景福门外另班行礼，钦此。

Imperial Edict

Issued October 19, 1908.

    The Grand Council in Audience has received Imperial commands for transmission to the Boart of Dependencies ordering that on the day of the feast to the Dalai Lama the latter shall receive and take leave of Their Imperial Majesties kneeling at the place of the repast. The Imperial commands were also issued to the Board of Dependencies and the Board of Rites through the Grand Council that the Dalai Lama shall make his ceremonial prostrations on the occasion of the birthday of Her Imperial Majesty outside the Ching Fu Gate, after the Princes and Ministers have concluded theirs.

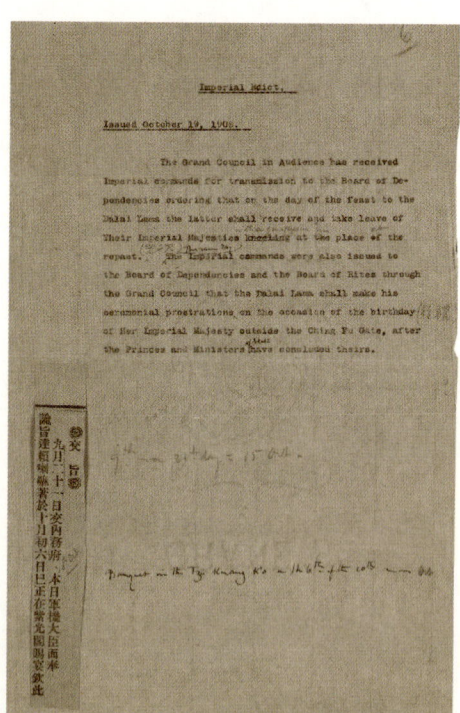

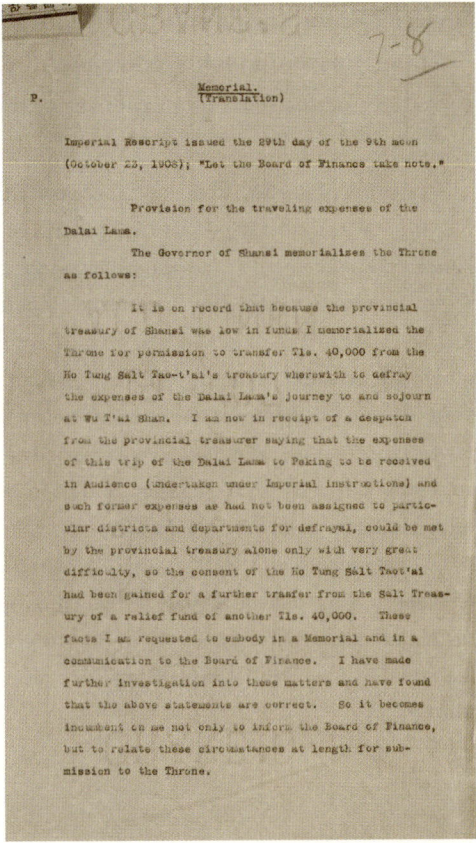

又奏拨解达赖喇嘛沿途开支银两片

再达赖喇嘛前赴五台山修养沿途一切开支款项前因司库款项支绌，奏明在河东道盐库内协拨银四万两在案。兹据布政使司详称，现在达赖遵旨进京陛见，所有各项开支及从前未发各州县垫款，司库独力难支，复经商准河东道，允于盐库正杂引课项下，再行拨解银四万两，以资凑济。详请奏资立案前来，臣复核无异。除咨明度支部查照外，理合附片具陈，伏乞圣鉴，谨奏。光绪三十四年九月二十九日奉朱批：度支部，知道，钦此。

Imperial Rescript Issued the 29th Day of the 9th Moon (Oct. 23, 1908)
"Let the Board of Finance take note"
Provision for the traveling expenses of the Dalai Lama

The governor of the Shansi memorializes the Throne as follows:

It is on record that because the provincial treasury of Shansi was low in funds I memorialized the Throne for permission to transfer Tls. 40,000 from the Ho Tung Salt Tao-T'ai's treasury wherewith to defray the expenses of the Dalai Lama's journey to and sojourn at Wu T'ai Shan. I am now in receipt of a dispatch from the provincial treasurer saying that the expenses of this trip of the Dalai Lama to Peking to be received in Audience (undertaken under Imperial instructions) and such former expenses as had not been assigned to particular districts and treasury alone only with very great difficulty, so the consent of the Ho Tung Salt Taot'ai had been gained for a further transfer from the Salt Treasury of a relief fund of another Tls. 40,000. These facts I am requested to embody in a Memorial and in a communication to the Board of Finance. I have made further investigation into these matters and have found that the above statements are correct. So it becomes incumbent on me not only to inform the Board of Finance, but to relate these circumstances at length for submission to the Throne.

又奏达赖喇嘛祝嘏礼节片

再九月二十五日准军机处片叫军机大臣面奉谕旨，达赖喇嘛祝嘏着于王大臣行礼后在景福门外另班行礼，钦此钦遵。到部恭照，本年十月初十日，慈禧端佑康颐昭豫庄诚寿恭钦献崇熙皇太后万寿圣节行礼时，预由理藩部官引达赖喇嘛于景福门外祗候俟，皇上率王大臣行礼后，理藩部引达赖喇嘛诣景福门阶下行三跪九叩礼，礼毕退出。谨附片奏闻。光绪三十四年十月初五日奉旨：知道了，钦此。

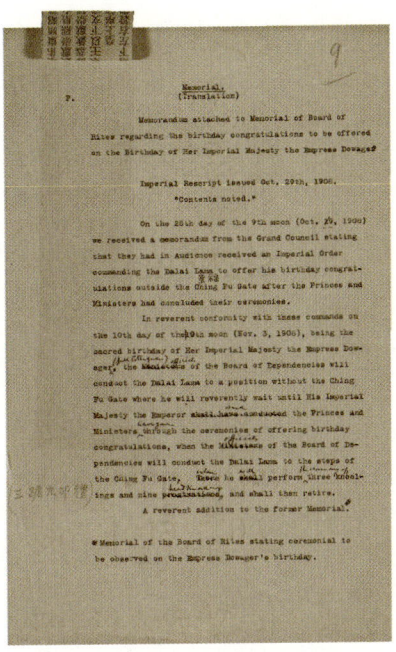

Memorial

Memorandum attached to Memorial of Board of Rites regarding the birthday congratulations to be offered on the Birthday of Her Imperial Majesty the Empress Dowager

Imperial Rescript Issued Oct. 29th, 1908

"Contents noted."

On the 25th day of the 9th moon (Oct. 9, 1908)

We received a memorandum from the Grand Council stating that they had in Audience received an Imperial Order commanding the Dalai Lama to offer his birthday congratulations outside the Ching Fu Gate after the Princes and Ministers had concluded their ceremonies.

In reverent conformity with these commands on the 10th day of the 10th moon (Nov. 3, 1908), being the sacred birthday of Her Imperial Majesty the Empress Dowager, the Ministers of the Board of Dependencies will conduct the Dalai Lama to a position without the Ching Fu Gate where he will reverently wait until His Imperial Majesty the Emperor and the Princes and Ministers have gone through the ceremonies of offering birthday congratulations, when the Ministers of the Board of Dependencies will conduct the Dalai Lama to the steps of the Ching Fu Gate, where he will perform the ceremony of three kneelings and nine prostrations, and shall then retire.

A reverent addition to the former Memorial.

Memorial of the Board of Rites stating ceremonial to be observed on the Empress Dowager's birthday.

奏折、谕旨

理藩部奏紫光阁赐宴达赖喇嘛应否跪迎跪送请旨遵行恭折仰祈圣鉴事

窃准内务府咨称，赐宴达赖喇嘛日期处所请旨，钦定一折，于光绪三十四年九月二十一日奉旨留中，钦此。嗣由军机处交出军机大臣面奉谕旨：达赖喇嘛着于十月初六日巳正在紫光阁赐宴，钦此。钦遵咨行前来，查臣部则例内开紫光阁赐宴，皇帝驾临，应行入坐人等俱在道旁按翼跪迎，皇帝还官均在道旁跪送等语。此次钦奉谕旨在紫光阁赐宴，皇上驾临，达赖喇嘛应否跪迎跪送，臣等未敢擅拟，谨声明定例，恭候钦定，一俟命下，臣等谨遵行所有。紫光阁赐宴达赖喇嘛应否跪迎跪送，请旨遵行缘由理合，恭折具陈，伏乞皇太后、皇上圣鉴训示。谨奏。

光绪三十四年九月二十五日奉旨已录。

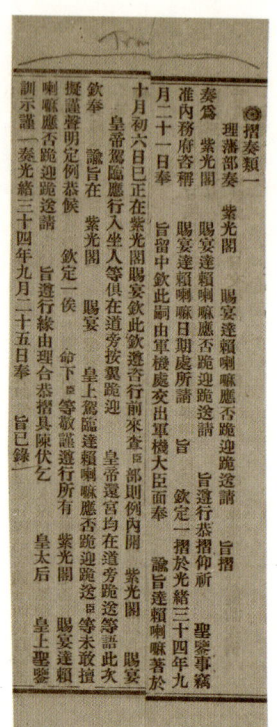

Memorial

Oct. 25, 1908

The Board of Dependencies memorializes the Throne asking whether the Dalai Lama shall or shall not, on the occasion of the Imperial Banquet in the Hall of Purple Light, kneel on the entrance and departure of His Imperial Majesty the Emperor. The Board reverently requests that the sacred glance may rest on their memorial and that the Imperial commands may be issued for their guidance.

We the Ministers are in receipt of a communication from the Department of the Imperial Household informing us that they had memorialized the Throne requesting that the time and place of the Imperial Banquet to be bestowed on the Dalai Lama be determined upon, and that on the twenty-first day of the ninth moon (October 15th) a Rescript had been issued commanding that the said memorial be laid aside for further consideration; that later, however, the members of the Grand Council transmitted Imperial commands received by them in Audience to the effect that an Imperial Banquet should be bestowed on the Dalai Lama in the Hall of Purple Light on the sixth day of the tenth moon (October 30th) at ten o'clock in the morning. They accordingly, in reverent obedience to the Imperial commands, apprised us of the above.

It is stated in the laws of this Board that when an Imperial Banquet is decreed in the Hall of Purple Light, all those entitled to be present at the Banquet shall kneel in two rows by the sides of the way when His Imperial Majesty enters and that on His Majesty's return to the Palace all shall likewise kneel. Such an Imperial Banquet has now been decreed and we, the Ministers, not daring of ourselves to decide as to whether the Dalai Lama shall or shall not kneel on the Imperial entrance and departure reverently cite the established rules and humbly await the issuance of an Imperial Mandate for our guidance.

We therefore venture in this reverent memorial to lay the matter of kneeling of the Dalai Lama at the Imperial Banquet in the Hall of Purple Light before the sacred glance of Their Imperial Majesties the Empress Dowager and the Emperor.

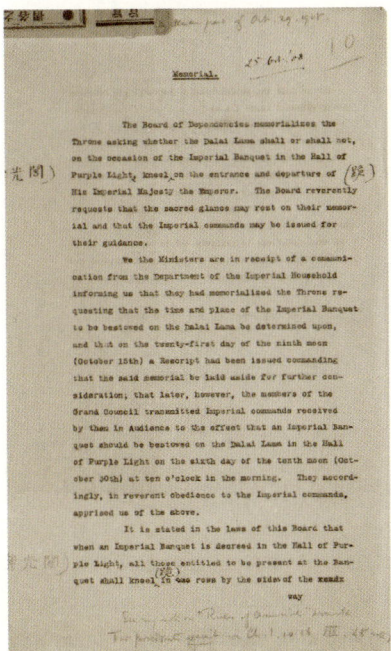
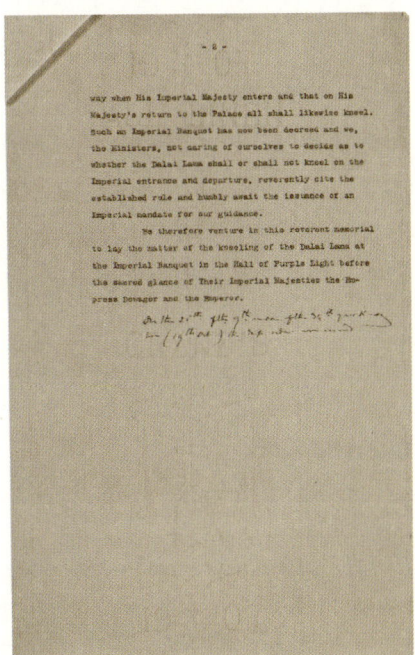

交旨

九月二十一日交内务府、本日军机大臣面奉谕旨：达赖喇嘛着于十月初
六日巳正在紫光阁赐宴，钦此。

谕旨

十月初十日内阁奉上谕：朕钦奉慈禧端佑
康颐昭豫庄诚寿恭钦献崇熙皇太后懿旨。
达赖喇嘛上月来京陛见，本日率徒祝嘏，
备抒悃忱，殊堪嘉尚，允宜特加封号，以
昭优异。达赖喇嘛业经循照从前旧制，封
为"西天大善自在佛"，兹特加封为"诚
顺赞化西天大善自在佛"，其敕封仪节，
着礼部、理藩部会同速议具奏。并按年赏
给年廪饩银一万两，由四川藩库分季支发。
达赖喇嘛受封后，即着仍回西藏，经过地
方该管官派员挨站护送，妥为照料。到藏
以后，务当恪遵主国之典章，奉扬中朝之
信义，并化导番众，谨守法度，习为善良。
所有事务依例报明驻藏大臣，随时转奏，
恭候定夺。期使疆圉永保治安，僧俗悉除
畛域，以无负朝廷护持黄教、绥靖边陲之
至意。并着理藩部传知达赖喇嘛祗领钦遵，
钦此。

Imperial Edict

Imperial Edict, issued November 3, 1908, issued by Her Imperial Majesty, the
Empress Dowager.

The Dalai Lama came to Peking last month and has had an Audience. Today he
has led his followers in the presentation of birthday congratulations in a sincere spirit
which We highly appreciate. We have determined to confer upon him an honorary title

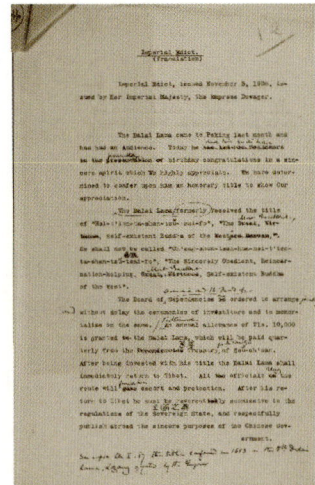
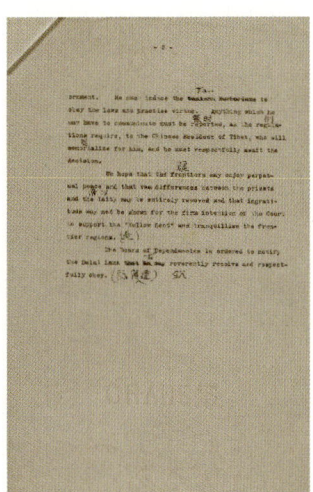

to show Our appreciation.

The Dalai Lama formerly received the title of "Hsi-t'ien-ta-shan-tzu-tsai-fo", "The Great, Virtuous, Self-existent Buddha of the Western Heaven". He shall now be called "Ch'eng-shun-tsan-hua-hsi-t'ien-ta-shan-tzu-tsai-fo", "The sincerely Obedient, Reincarnation-helping, Great, Virtuous, Self-existent Buddha of the West".

The Board of Dependencies is ordered to arrange without delay the ceremonies of investiture and to memorialize on the same. An annual allowance of T1s. 10,000 is granted to the Dalai Lama, which will be paid quarterly from the Treasury of Ssu-ch'uan. After being invested with his title the Dalai Lama shall immediately return to Tibet. All the officials on the route will give escort and protection. After his return to Tibet he must be reverently submissive to the regulations of the Sovereign State and respectfully publish abroad the sincere purposes of the Chinese Government. He must induce the Western Barbarians to obey the laws and practice virtue. Anything which he may have to communicate must be reported, as the regulations require, to the Chinese Resident of Tibet, who will memorialize for him, and he must respectfully await the decision.

We hope that the frontiers may enjoy perpetual peace and that the differences between the priests and the laity may be entirely removed and that ingratitude may not be shown for the firm intention of the Court to support the "Yellow Sect" and tranquillize the frontier regions.

The Board of Dependencies is ordered to notify the Dalai Lama that he may reverently receive and respectfully obey.

圣旨

（译文）

阴历十月廿六号（1908 年 11 月 19 号）
转交理藩部。

当天，理藩部代表达赖喇嘛呈送奏折，
询问他何时可以与追随者一道前往梓宫
前吊唁刚刚驾崩的太皇太后（即孝钦显
皇后叶赫那拉氏，慈禧太后）和光绪皇
帝陛下。喇嘛已收到回复，要求他在当
月廿七日（即 1908 年 11 月 20 号）上
午九点到十一点之间前去吊唁。

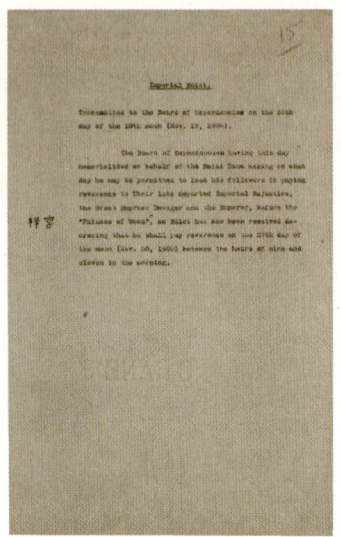

Imperial Edict

Transmitted to the Board of Dependencies on the 26th day of the 10th moon (Nov.19, 1906).

The Board of Dependencies having this day memorialized on behalf of the Dalai Lama asking on what day he may be permitted to lead his followers in paying reverence to Their late departed Imperial Majesties, the Great Empress Dowager and the Emperor, before the "Palace of Wood", an Edict has now been received decreeing that he shall pay reverence on the 27th day of the moon (Nov. 20, 1908) between the hours of nine and eleven in the morning.

圣旨

（译文）

阴历十一月六日（1908 年 11 月 29 日），以下奏折呈送理藩部和内务府：

今日，军机处大臣收到圣旨。圣旨上陈：达赖喇嘛作为堪布（即住持之意）首领和各寺庙喇嘛的首领，（对先帝）尽职尽责，殊堪嘉奖。因此，达赖喇嘛被赐予二十条哈达、十匹绸缎、十匹礼仪用绸缎、四对大荷包、四对小荷包，手下堪布及徒众两千两银子；各寺庙喇嘛加三个月俸禄。

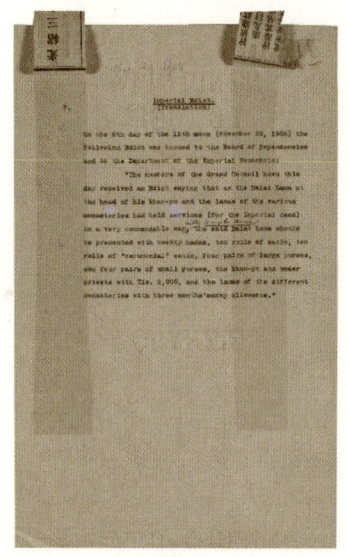

Imperial Edict

On the 6th day of the 11th moon (November 29, 1908) the following Edict was issued to the Board of Dependencies and to the Department of the Imperial Household:

"The members of the Grand Council have this day received and Edict saying that as the Dalai Lama at the head of his Khan-pu and the lamas of the various monasteries had held services (for the Imperial dead) in a very commendable way, the said Dalai Lama should be presented with twenty hadas, ten rolls of satin, ten rolls of "ceremonial" satin, four pairs of large purses, and four pairs of small purses, the Khan-pu and under priests with T1s. 2,000, and the lamas of the different monasteries with three month's money allowance."

圣旨

（译文）

1908 年 12 月 16 日敕旨

关于达赖喇嘛启程返回西藏事件，由理藩部堂官博迪苏陪同前往保定府。他所到之处的所有巡抚和将军都要任命高级官员为其提供护送和保卫。

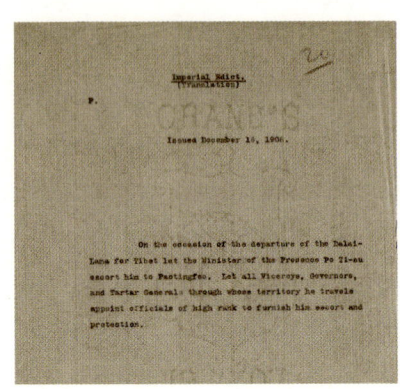

Imperial Edict

Issued December 16, 1908

On the occasion of the departure of the Dalai Lama for Tibet let the Minister of the Presence Po Ti-su escort him to Paotingfoo. Let all Viceroys, Governors, and Tartar Generals through whose territory he travels appoint officials of high rank to furnish him escort and protection.

阴历十一月廿五日（1908 年 12 月 18 日），理藩部上呈奏折，大意是：达赖喇嘛希望与追随者一道前往喇嘛庙礼拜。

朝廷批复："已阅，已同意。"

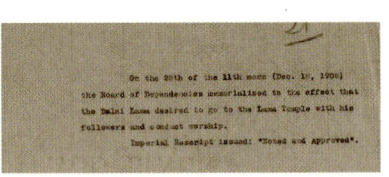

On the 25th of the 11th moon (Dec. 18, 1908) the Board of Dependencies memorialized to the effect that the Dalai Lama desired to go to the Lama Temple with his followers and conduct worship.

Imperial Rescript issued: "Noted and Approved".

阴历十一月廿六日（1908年12月19日），理藩部代表达赖喇嘛上呈奏折，请求将一些堪布留在北京，担任唐古忒语（藏语）老师。同时，再从西藏派遣一些年轻人前往北京，学习汉语。

朝廷批复："同意。"

On the 26th of the 11th moon (Dec. 19, 1908) the Board of Dependencies memorialized on behalf of the Dalai Lama asking that some K'an-pu be left in Peking to act as Teachers of T'angut, and that some lads be sent from Tibet to Peking to study Chinese.

Imperial Rescript issued: "Granted".

同一天，理藩部代表达赖喇嘛上呈奏折，感谢皇恩浩荡，并附呈一尊佛像和一方黄色哈达。

朝廷批复："已阅，收下佛像和哈达。"

On the same day the Board of Dependencies memorialized on behalf of the Dalai Lama returning thanks for the Imperial grace and presenting one Buddha and one yellow hada.

Imperial Rescript issued: "Noted. Let the Buddha and the hada be received."

奏折

达寿（理藩部左侍郎）撰折，就朝廷要求他们护送达赖喇嘛离京事宜作出回复。朝廷于阴历十一月廿九日（1908年12月22日）下诏回复，称"已阅"。

理藩部撰折，大意是达赖喇嘛于阴历十一月廿八日（1908年12月21日）离开北京，前往西宁和塔尔寺。他们全体护送他及随行人员前行。朝廷于阴历十一月廿九日（1908年12月22日）批复，称"已阅"。

Memorial

Ta-shou (Vice President of the Board of Dependencies) having memorialized in response to the Imperial commands ordering them to escort the Dalai Lama on his departure from Peking, an Imperial Rescript was issued on the 20th of the 11th Moon (December 22, 1908) as follows:

"Noted."

The Board of Dependencies having memorialized to the effect that the Dalai Lama left Peking on the 28th of the 11th Moon (December 21, 1908) to proceed to Hsi-ning and T'a-er-ssu and that they escorted him in a body. Imperial Rescript issued on the 29th of the 11th Moon (December 22, 1908)

"Noted."

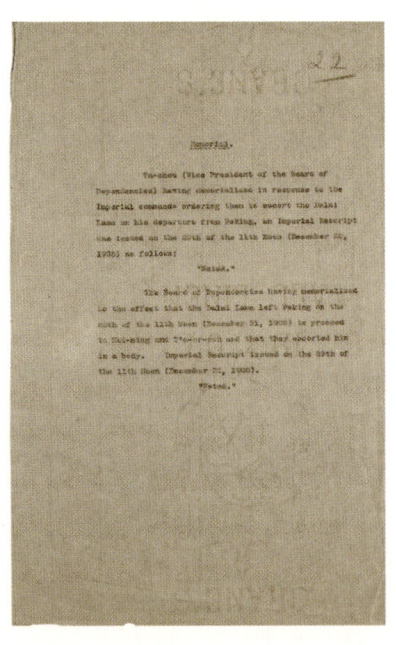

（四）英文剪报

The Visit of the Dalai Lama to Peking

July 22, 1908

　　An Imperial Edict issued on the 20th inst. states that as everything has been settled in Tibet between China and Great Britain, the Throne now orders that the Dalai Lama come up to Peking for Imperial audience, under the protection of a body of Chinese officials and soldiers.

　　It is believed that the Dalai Lama will proceed up to Peking in September next.

达赖喇嘛访京

　　1908 年 7 月 22 日

　　20 日朝廷发布诏书称，大清朝与大英帝国之间有关西藏的一切事务都已安排妥当。朝廷命令达赖喇嘛进京觐见，由全体汉族官员和护卫护送。据信，达赖喇嘛将会在次年九月抵京。

The DALAI LAMA[1]

From a correspondent

Peking, September 28.

达赖喇嘛 [2]

通讯记者报道

9 月 28 日，发自北京

Arrival in Peking

抵京

The long delayed arrival of the Dalai Lama took place to-day. His train

---

[1]　North China Daily News, Oct. 5, 1908.

[2]　1908 年 10 月 5 日，《字林西报》（前身是《北华捷报》）。

was expected at the Belgian station shortly after 1:30 p.m. and, a good three-quarters of an hour before that time, a large crowd of Chinese had collected in the open space between the station-yard and the Tsien Men. They stood in a closely packed semi-circle, held together, like a large blue bundle, by a yellow cordon of khaki-clad police. Most Europeans took up positions on the walls, and nearly all were armed with cameras. It was a brilliantly fine morning, with a cloudless sky, and a sun that turned the roofs of the Imperial Palace to pale gold, and drew a faint shimmer of heat from the hills. On the platform, two, orange-colored standards of the Lu-chun waved above either end of a line of piled arms, and, outside the station yard, a guard of honors stood at ease, springing to attention every now and then to salute officials driven past in closed carriages. Inside the compound row of shaggy ponies, with heavy Chinese saddles, and trappings of scarlet, yellow, and red were hold in readiness in front of a crowd of blue-hooded Peking carts.

今天，达赖喇嘛终于抵京。这一刻已经拖延了太久。他乘坐的火车预计将会在午后一时半左右抵达车站。在 45 分钟之前，就已经有一大群中国人聚集在站场和前门之间的空地上。他们围成了一个密不透风的半圆形，紧紧站在一起。穿着卡其色制服的警察用黄色警戒带把他们围住，就像捆扎一大捆蓝色的货物。大多数欧洲人爬到墙上，手里几乎都举着照相机。那天早晨风和日丽，万里无云。在阳光的映照下，故宫屋顶发出柔和的金黄色光芒，又从远处的小山上吸收了微弱的热光。在站台上，有一堆武器。在这堆武器的前后端，各有一条橙色的军旗在迎风飘扬。在站场外，一个仪仗队正在稍息。他们时不时迅速立正站好，向坐着有篷马车经过的官员行礼致敬。这个仪仗队里的小马毛发都很蓬松散乱，也都配有沉重的马鞍子和深红色、黄色和红色的马饰。这些都已准备就绪。身后是很多带有着蓝顶子的北京式马车。

As the half hour approached, the order was given to unpile arms, and shortly afterwards the train steamed into the station. There rolled out of it, wave upon wave, a sea of human beings as barbaric, yet picturesque, as any I have seen outside Drury Lane Theatre at Christmas time. In describing it, I distain strict accuracy, without fearing any exaggeration. For, at first, the station seemed a tangled skein with threads of every conceivable color, crossed and intertwining—as though some color-blind showman were playing a gigantic, and complicated, game of "cat's cradle". Then gradually, the medley disengaged, thinned, and lengthened into processional column, headed by mounted standard-bearers wearing scarlet hats, shaped like large tulips. Behind them, rode six drummers, beating in strict, slow time, with elaborate flourish if black sticks, on drums either side of their saddles. Next came a body of men whose dark eyes and swarthy faces looked darker still under wide, brass helmets, flat and burnished. They wore flowing capes of red, yellow and purple and rode unkempt, sturdy, little ponies with long manes and tails. A troop of mounted infantry with drawn swords, modern drilled, preceded four mounted buglers heralding the approach of the great yellow chair in which the Lama sat curtained from view, borne by some twenty carriers, eight at whom actually supported the chair, though the remainder made a brave show of straining, six each side, beneath a couple of ropes resting lightly on their shoulders. Behind the chair was carried what I can only call an enormous yellow sunshade, since it was too small to be turned a canopy, yet too splendid, surely, to be dubbed umbrella. But, bien entendu, it was very magnificent indeed, not stiff, nor plain, nor ordinary, but rich, long-skirted and majestically waving. A smaller one bore it company, not nearly so impressive, yet gorgeously spangled, and glittering like the dress of a harlequin. The rear of the procession was brought up by thirty or forty priests, swathed from shoulder to ankle in thick, chocolate-colored blankets, with close-cropped heads and clean-shaven copper-brown faces. They looked like a group of monks brought back to life from the pages of the *Canterbury Tales*, and gave a touch of medievalism in harmony with the towering gray walls through which the procession swept, whilst, just at the right moment, to

add a touch of romance, loosely-clad, clattering horsemen galloped along its
flanks.

时间接近一点半，车站接到命令，把武器分散放开。很快火车就进
站了。从火车上涌下大量乘客。人山人海。车站顿时热闹起来。一副混
乱但壮观的场景，就像圣诞节期间我在伦敦特鲁里街剧院外看到的一模
一样。要描述这个场景，我就不严格按照准确原则了。请允许我夸大一
些。首先，车站看起来纷乱如丝，充斥着各种你能够想到的颜色。他们
向不同方向穿梭、交织着。看起来就像有些患有色盲的杂耍艺人正在玩
一个巨大而复杂的"猫的摇篮"游戏。接着，慢慢地，混合的人群自由
散去，逐渐变稀、变长，形成了整齐的专业队列。队伍的领头者是骑在
马上的旗手们。他们戴着深红色的帽子，帽子的形状就像一朵朵巨大的
郁金香花。在旗手身后，是六位鼓手。他们严格按照鼓点，慢慢地敲打
着。鼓槌儿是黑色的，带有精美的华饰。在马鞍的两侧各挂有一面鼓。
接着，后面是一大群人。他们都长着乌黑的眼睛，黝黑的脸庞在宽大铜
头盔的映照下看起来更黑。他们的头盔可是擦得锃亮。他们穿着红黄紫
色相间的披风，披风迎风摇摆。他们的坐骑都是小马，毛发蓬乱，却很
结实。马鬃和马尾都很长。一队骑马步兵举着抽出鞘的宝剑。能看得出，
他们接受的是现代方式的操练。他们后面是四位骑马的喇叭手，为身后
一乘黄色大轿子开路。喇嘛坐在轿子里，轿帘放下。大约有二十个轿夫
抬着轿子。实际上，只有八个人在用着劲儿。剩下的轿夫分别站在轿子
的两侧，每侧有六名。他们做出非常用力的样子，为队伍造势。其实，
两条绳子只是轻轻地搭在他们肩膀上。在椅子后面，人们抬着一件物品。
我只能将其称为一把巨大的黄色遮阳伞。因为它的大小还算不上是华盖。
同时它又是如此豪华耀眼，当然更不能简单地称为伞。当然了，毫无疑
问，这个巨大的遮阳伞富丽堂皇，还带有边缘，既不呆板僵硬，也不素
朴平常。它就是那样华贵、宏伟地在风中飘荡着。旁边还有个小点儿的

遮阳伞，虽然不那么耀眼，但也装饰有亮闪闪的优美饰物。在阳光的映照下，就像花斑眼镜蛇的衣裳那么五彩缤纷、金光闪闪。整个队伍的后方是三四十名僧侣。他们从肩膀到脚踝处都紧紧裹着厚厚的、巧克力颜色的毯子。他们头发剪得极短，脸庞呈古铜色，胡子刮得很干净。这一队僧侣看起来就像是从《坎特伯雷故事集》里走出来的一样，给人一种中世纪遗风的感觉。这种感觉和沿途经过的灰色高墙相得益彰。同时，在这一队僧侣的两翼还疾驰着衣着宽松的骑兵，更是增添了一丝传奇色彩，笃笃的马蹄声在空气中回响着。

The route from the Tsien Men to the An-ding Men is, practically, straight, and I followed the procession, through the city, out on to the plain. The road was lined on either side by a crowd, in places, five or six rows deep and, as I was on foot, I was caught, here and there, in a whirl pool of struggling perspiring Chinese. But the scene on the plain repaid perseverance. The procession at some point or other, had been met by fresh contingents, by another body of priests, of instance, who marched on foot, wearing those extraordinary Caesarian-looking helmets, made I should hazard, of cardboard, and ornamented with tufts of wool, which you may see any day, during service, in the Lama Temple. The country, between the city wall and the yellow Temple, is used as a golf course, and is wide, treeless, and billowy, like an English down. Picture the extraordinary procession winding slowly across it, drums beating, bugles blowing, with the sun in a blue sky shining upon vivid colors and glittering swords. It was worth seeing, but one gave a gasp of delight as one neared the Temple. There, in front of its entrance, stood long-robed priests, facing one another in yellow rows, like giant daffodils against a back-ground of green trees, given suddenly to view by opening doors: for, just as the head of the column began to cross the arched, white-stone bridge opposite them, the massive iron gates swung back and showed the Temple grounds. They waited thus, these priests, the breeze fluttering their gowns, whilst the procession of scarlet and blue, and yellow that matched their own, filed up between them, and as the end of it swept leftward out of sight, they closed, and moved together into the circle of green. Then the big gray gates swung to again... The Lama's long journey was ended, and the crowd, standing fast for a few moments, broke up and returned home.

从前门到安定门的路线几乎是一条直线。我跟在整个队伍的后面，穿过北京城，出城来到空旷的平原上。道路两旁都拥挤地站着一大群人，有些地方甚至围得里三层外三层。我是步行，所以身不由己地被大汗淋漓涌动的人潮从这儿挤到那儿。不过，平地上的景象却不枉我费了这么大的劲儿。不知在什么时候，队伍中又新加入了小分队。比方说，我看到了一大群步行前进的和尚。他们都戴着那种凯撒大帝式的头盔。我敢打赌，这种头盔是用硬纸板做成的，装饰着簇簇羊毛。不管什么时候，在喇嘛庙里的宗教仪式中，你都能见到这种头盔。城墙和黄色的庙宇之间的地区被用作了高尔夫球场。这片区域很开阔，没长树木，土如波浪般起伏翻滚，像英国的开阔高地。设想一下，这个最非比寻常的行进队伍缓缓地穿过这片地区，鼓点震天、号角呼啸。蓝天白云，灿烂的阳光下映射出数不清鲜艳的色彩和金光闪闪的刀剑。这场景真的值得一看。不过，你离寺庙越近，就越惊叹、越欣喜。在庙门前，穿着黄色长袍的僧人面对面站着，就像巨大的水仙花映衬在绿树下。突然之间庙门一开，豁然开朗。队伍的排头开始越过庙门对面的拱形白石头桥。厚重的铁门向后打开，寺庙的一派洞天映入眼帘。这些僧侣就这样静候着。微风吹起他们的僧袍。那个红、蓝、黄颜色相得益彰的队伍从僧人中间鱼贯而入。队伍尾部向左扫过，之后闭合，又一同朝着绿色的圆圈移动。接着，灰色的大门再次转动。喇嘛的行进队伍总算过去了。看热闹的人群仍旧屹立在原地。过了一会儿，大家才散去，各自回家。

VISITS OF THE DALAI LAMA AND TASHI LAMA TO PEKING
(FROM OUR OWN CORRESPONDENT)

PEKING, MAY 10.

达赖喇嘛和班禅喇嘛访京

本报记者报道，5 月 10 日，北京

Much interest is manifested here at the expected visit to the capital this year of the two highest spiritual authorities in Tibet, the Dalai Lama and the Tashi Lama. The Dalai Lama is at present residing at Wutai-shan, within five days' journey of Peking, and is living in a monastery in great state and within a large retinue. He has sent greetings to several of the foreign Ministers in Peking, notably to the American, who is a recognized authority on Tibetan Buddhism, and to the German, who sent him a portrait of the Emperor William.

公众对于今年西藏两位最高精神领袖——达赖喇嘛和班禅喇嘛拟访京事宜表现出了极大的兴趣。目前，达赖喇嘛停驻五台山。此地距离北京大概有五天的路程。他居住在一座庄严宏伟的寺庙里，扈从甚重、守卫森严。他已经派人向北京的几位大使送上了问候与祝福，尤其包括在藏传佛教方面被视为公认权威的美国人和给他送去威廉一世肖像画的德国人。

For some time past the Dalai Lama has had no foreign advisor. His former advisor and private secretary was the Tibetan scholar, the Rev. Teramoto, a Japanese, who resided with him in Kumban monastery, near Sining, and returned last year to Japan in ill-health. He arrived at Peking on Thursday and will shortly rejoin the Dalai Lama. Should the Dalai Lama come for an audience, as is expected, he will be received with equal honor to that shown to his only predecessor to visit this capital, the fifth Dalai Lama, who arrived in the reign of Shun-che, the first emperor of the present dynasty, and spent here the winter of 1652.

189

在过去的一段时间里，达赖喇嘛没有外国顾问。他之前的顾问和私人秘书是一位西藏学者，日本人寺本大师。这位大师曾和喇嘛一道住在西宁附近的塔尔寺，去年因为健康状况不佳返回了日本。不过周四他也抵达了北京，将会与达赖喇嘛短暂会晤。正如预期的，如果达赖喇嘛希望觐见，朝廷就会像接见之前访京的他唯一的前任五世达赖喇嘛一样，赋予同样的尊荣。1652 年的冬天，五世达赖喇嘛曾在清朝首位皇帝顺治帝在位期间访京。

The Tashi Lama, who was received by the Prince of Wales at Rawalpindi on December 7, 1905, recently memorialized the Throne from Shigatse, praying for permission to come to Peking and be received in audience, which was granted. The memorial was, no doubt, in the Oriental way, prompted from the Throne. It is expected that he will come via Calcutta, and that he will also be shown great honor, as was his predecessor who visited the Emperor Keen-lung on the occasion of his 70th birthday, when the emperor proceeded to Jehol to await his arrival and accompanied him to Peking, where he died on November 27th, 1780.

1905 年，12 月 7 日，班禅喇嘛在拉瓦尔品第（巴基斯坦北部城市）受到威尔士亲王的接见。班禅喇嘛最近从日喀则向朝廷呈递奏折，请求朝廷允许他前往京城觐见皇帝。这一请求得到了准许。毫无疑问，这份奏折实际上是在朝廷敦促下呈递的。这是一种东方特色。人们预测，他会从印度的加尔各答经过。朝廷也会赋予他无上的尊荣。因为在乾隆帝七十大寿时，班禅喇嘛的前任也曾前来拜寿。当时，乾隆帝向热河进发，等候班禅的到来，并和他一道前往北京。1780 年 11 月 27 日，那位班禅喇嘛病逝于北京。

It is well known that China desires to reorganize her methods of administration in Tibet with a view to securing greater government control. Two recent decrees speaking of Tibet as "the real frontier of

China" explain that the unusual appointment of Chao Erh-fung as Imperial Residents in Tibet and of his brother Chao Erh-hsun, as Viceroy of the adjoining province Sze-chwan, was designed with object of ensuring harmonious cooperation in developing military efficiency, encouraging education and agriculture, and generally improving the government of Tibet. The officials specially selected for service in Tibet are promised a long tenure of office. The necessary funds and officials will be provided from the rich province of Sze-chwan, the Viceroy Chao Erh-hsun being the ablest financier and one of the most upright administrators in the Empire. In time China aspires to reconstruct Tibet into another province of the Empire, therein following the precedent of the New Dominion which, in accordance with Imperial decree of September 5th, 1882, was given a provincial administration like the 18 provinces of China proper.

众所周知，清政府希望整顿对藏管理事务，以便加强政府管理。最近的两项法案都将西藏称为"中国的真正领土"，并解释了将赵尔丰任命为驻藏大臣、将其兄弟赵尔巽任命为西藏邻省四川省总督的不同寻常之处。朝廷的目的是确保和谐发展、相互合作、提高军事效能、促进教育和农业发展，并从整体上促进健全西藏治理。朝廷专门选派了官员负责以上事项，长期任职。必要的资金和官员储备将由富庶的天府之国四川提供。而赵尔巽总督也是大清国最具才能的户部尚书和最正直的行政官员。届时，大清王朝希望将西藏重建为帝国的重要一省。朝廷遵循之前开辟新疆土的先例，按照 1882 年 9 月 5 日颁布的圣谕，西藏和中国内陆的十八个省一样，也设置行省管理。

Oct. 12, 1908 (*North China Daily News*)
1908 年 10 月（《字林西报》）

THE DALAI LAMA evidently wants to stand on his dignity. He has demanded that the place where he is to be given an Imperial Audience shall be in the Chients'ing Throne room and that when entering the Palace he shall be preceded by two eunuchs carrying incense burners. Their Majesties have refused the first but granted the second request in view of the Pontiff's sacred character. We may state in explanation that the Chients'ing Throne room is the usual audience hall for Ambassadors and that the Emperor, Empress and Empress Dowager have the prerogative of being preceded by eunuchs carrying incense burners. The Dalai Lama's place of audience, we understand, will be the Jênshou Hall and the date fixed for the audience is the 14th instant. H. E. Chang Yin-t'ang, late Vice Imperial Resident at Lhasa, and a Manchu high official named Ta Shou are in daily attendance on the Dalai Lama, with whom there have been frequent secret conferences on Tibetan matters which are to be explained by the Dalai Lama to their Majesties during his audience.

达赖喇嘛显然认为自己应受到应有的礼遇。他一直提出自己觐见皇帝的地方应该是乾清宫。而且在他进入乾清宫时，应由两位手持香炉的太监在前方引领。皇帝和皇太后陛下拒绝了第一个要求，但考虑到教宗的神圣地位准许了第二个请求。我们也许解释过，乾清宫是各国大使通常觐见皇帝的地方。皇帝、皇后和皇太后才有特权由手持香炉的太监引领进入此地。我们知道，达赖喇嘛的觐见地点应该是颐和园仁寿殿。达赖喇嘛觐见日期确定为本月 14 日。拉萨上一届查办藏事的副都统、外务部张丞堂荫棠和一位满族高级官员理藩部左侍郎达寿每日陪伴在达赖喇嘛左右。他们之间频繁进行了秘密会谈，商讨西藏事宜。而在未来的觐见中达赖喇嘛将会向皇帝陛下陈述这些事宜。